Our company, AT&T, is dedicated to being a global leader in information services and products. To some observers, such dedication conjures up little more than fierce competition, all-out pursuit of customers, and eyes firmly -- and only -- on the bottom line.

Dee Dee Torrell offers a view of the marketplace that focuses on a different and likewise important aspect of corporate governance -- its humanity. We are, when all is said and done, a company of people, linked together in success or failure. Our ability to understand, to support and to care about one another is critical to the success of our far-flung business.

This book is an important contribution to a better understanding of the business environment. It reminds us that personal commitment to treating people with respect is not in conflict with our success; on the contrary, treating people with respect is <u>essential</u> to business success.

At AT&T, we are proud of the way we treat one another, in good times or bad. And we are proud of people like Dee Dee Torrell, who are living proof that even in a large organization, one individual can make an enormous difference.

William V. Catucci, AT&T Vice President, Government Affairs

I0892105

The business of business is not business – at least, not for Christians and for other men and women of good faith. The business of business is people: customers, supervisors, fellow employees, investors, suppliers, even competitors. In *Heart-Business*, Dee Dee Torrell explores the human side of business from the inside of AT&T. With empathy and insight she reflects on the difficulties and the payoffs of bringing the dignity of the individual back into the marketplace. This is a useful book, full of provocative examples, suggestions and questions for study and reflection.

Gregory F. Augustine Pierce, former president, National Center for the Laity

Dee Dee Torrell captures the essence of the needs for competitive business success in the future. Organizations and managers must recognize the unique difference of each individual and provide a nurturing and supportive environment which values that difference and allows each employee to maximize his or her potential.

Larry Garfinkel, AT&T Vice President, Marketing Services Organization

In today's rapidly changing global environment, positive recognition of an individual's self-worth, positive social relations within the workplace, and positive linkages between an employee's work life and home life are essential for a successful corporate and social future. In fact, all are essential to enhancing positive employee relations.

Dee Dee Torrell points out that the segmentation and separation of employee's work and personal lives are not productive. In *Heart-Business* she examines these issues and adds an essential component--a positive moral and ethical dimension designed to enhance employee empowerment.

Harvey Kahalas, Dean and Professor of Management,
University of Lowell, College of Management Science, and President, HKE Inc.

Heart-Business

Building a Kinder, Gentler Workplace

Dolores Lynn Torrell

Resurrection Press
Mineola • New York

Dedication:

To Mom, Dad, Debra and Bob
for their love and support of me

To the faculty and students at Immaculate Conception Seminary, Seton Hall University,
who have taught me so much about God's love

and to the employees at AT&T, with love.

First published in 1991 by Resurrection Press, Ltd.
P.O. Box 248
Williston Park, NY 11596

Second Printing — October 1992

Edited by and Study Questions devised by Nancy Benvenga

"Think People" designed by Mike DelCasino for WRS

Shared Values pyramid reprinted with permission from AT&T Consumer Products' *Challenge*

ISBN 1-878718-07-X
Library of Congress Catalog Number 91-62219

Cover by John Murello

Printed in the United States of America.

Acknowledgments

I extend my appreciation to a number of people who have contributed in one way or another to the writing of this book. First, to Nancy Benvenga, my editor at Resurrection Press, who provided support and friendship as well as professional editing skill. Secondly, to John Leonardi, my publisher, and his wife Mary, who shared with me their enthusiasm about my manuscript and offered words of encouragement throughout the process of writing. Next, to my good friend Cynthia McCoy, with her gracious serving spirit, who read and often reread material, and who along with my other dear friend Susanna Palmer offered valuable suggestions. Finally, to Sister Concetta Russo; to Ted Harvey, my Director at AT&T, who supported my writing of this book; to Larry Garfinkel, Bill Catucci, Marie Santana, Bob Ettl, Mike Murphy, Mike DelCasino, Dr. Zeni Fox, Dr. Bill Toth, Rev. Diana Dale, Stella Wilkins, Eileen McNamara-Raisch, Ken Bertaccini, Dr. Larry Goldfarb, Rick Cain, Katherine Bakes, "AT&T's mail clerk" Harriet, Bob Geller – and Mr. Bob Allen, Chairman and CEO of AT&T.

Contents

Foreword

In his encyclical *Laborem Exercens*, Pope John Paul II provided the world with a profound and extensive meditation on the importance of work. Work, he affirmed, is "the key to the social question." It humanizes and socializes us for better or worse. Most importantly, our work is the critical setting in which we can choose to be empowered by divine graciousness or trapped by demonic determinisms. The stakes are indeed high. In the concluding paragraphs of this encyclical, Pope John Paul invited all Christians to begin the noble task of examining the theological, spiritual and ethical dimensions of work.

This small volume by Dee Dee Torrell stands as an important and valuable response to Pope John Paul's invitation. As a working manager in a major corporation and a trained pastoral minister, Ms. Torrell knows well the dyings and risings that occur daily in the marketplace. In simple and direct language she probes the "heart" of our work experience, calling upon us to be ministers of honest compassion in the workplace. Through a skillful telling of personal narratives, she outlines the service dimensions of workplace ministry. It is a ministry that seeks to empower people to view their work as an extension of God's creative and compassionate action in the world. It is modeled after the personal example of Jesus who encountered people in the highways and byways of their lives. Finally, it is grounded in obedience to God and respect for self, neighbor and environment.

If the workplace is commonly perceived as a battleground for profits in which morally unencumbered individuals compete for dominative power, Ms. Torrell offers an alternate vision, namely, the workplace as a caring community in which people bond themselves to each other in supportive trust and kindness. Today in response to the work of Dee Dee

Torrell and other Christian ministers in the marketplace, a new bottom line realism is emerging in today's business centers. It is a realism that steadfastly refuses to choose between people and profits. Moreover, it is a realism grounded in the indisputable fact that people as well as businesses flourish in contexts of trust and respect.

I commend this book to all the prophetic realists in our midst, especially those who seek to extend the justice, joy and peace of God's reign to our workplaces.

Dr. William J. Toth, Assistant Professor of Moral Theology
School of Theology, Seton Hall University

Letter on The Dignity of Work to AT&T's *Focus* Magazine

I COMMEND you on your articles that feature the personal side of the business. I have been deeply concerned about the morale of employees, and your magazine is one effort to help lift the spirit at AT&T.

In the twelve years I have worked at AT&T, I have seen a decline in our respect and caring for one another – what I once saw coined the "dignity of work." Together we have been through the frustration of divestiture, numerous reorganization efforts, and increasing demand for excellence against a competitive industry. Yet through it all we have forgotten how to interact with one another as people – working as a team toward a common mission – to make AT&T the world leader in telecommunications.

However, we can also be a world-leading company in our humanity with all employees at every level. We used to be. True, we have outstanding benefits, a good medical and TLC department, a new AT&T employee career pathing program and outside community efforts such as the Pioneer group and United Way. We have had a steady stream of employee attitude surveys to deal with the morale problem. However, those surveys deal with statistics, not people.

In addition to my position at AT&T, I am a pastoral minister and counselor. The number of employees who have expressed to me their disenchantment over the way we treat one another is overwhelming. I am moved deeply to see how many people want to be more caring, more concerned with their fellow person, but often are viewed by others as weak for their attempts. We all are under pressure to achieve. One can rightly argue that pressure at work today is much greater because work has become more competitive and complex. Often we end up short-cutting the dignity of work.

How often do we look beyond our jobs to the human dimensions of our work? Do we answer a telephone, respond to a memo or interact with each other differently because we consider our work more than a job – in fact, a career, a "vocation"? How much flexibility do we reflect in such matters as to ensure that the personal health and well-being and family life of our peers and subordinates are protected and respected? Do we encourage a balance between work and personal life? Do we take the time to get to know one another as people? What are our dreams, goals, interests and sorrows?

For AT&T to compete as the world leader in business, we need to be competitive, aggressive, attentive in our work and strive for excellence. But competition is not synonymous with meanness toward our fellow human being. Let's be a role model for corporations and a world leader in the dignity of work. Let's be a reminder to all to dig down deep and rediscover the principles that promote the dignity of work.

Dee Dee Torrell
March 14, 1989

Chapter One

A Marketplace Devoid of Spirituality

The purpose of a business firm is not simply to make a profit, but is to be found in its very existence as a community of persons who in various ways are endeavoring to satisfy their basic needs, and who form a particular group at the service of the whole of society. Profit is a regulator of the life of a business, but it is not the only one; other human and moral factors must also be considered which, in the long term, are at least equally important for the life of a business.

— JOHN PAUL II[1]

Tom

On a late, sunny Friday afternoon everyone was winding down from a busy work week and looking forward to the weekend. Tom was not particularly excited about going home, for he would be spending his weekend consoling his children and himself over the loss of their mother. Two weeks before, Tom's wife had left him and the children for a "new life" with another man she had met at her office.

Tom is a manager who worked twenty years for his company. He has consistently received bonuses throughout the years and periodically won recognition awards for some of his ideas. He also received high praise from his coworkers and subordinates for his kindness, humor and compassion. As a Christian, Tom tries to live his faith in the workplace through helping others. He is a devoted family man who enjoys many recreational activities with his family. His wife's leaving was indeed a great shock to him. Work had become Tom's solace.

Tom shared his family problems with Bill, his supervisor, letting Bill know that he may need some extra time for a while to spend with his children until things settled at home. Tom's children were teenagers, which made caring for them a little easier, but he was concerned about the emotional scars their mother's leaving would have on them, especially since these were the sensitive years for growing children.

As Tom was finishing his work and getting ready to leave for home that Friday afternoon, Bill appeared at the door. Bill seemed a bit nervous and somewhat distant.

"Tom," said Bill, "as you heard in our staff meeting today with the Vice President, this department is going to go through some reorganizing quite soon, and we need to downsize our divisions. I am sorry to tell you, but your division is going to be dissolved as of five o'clock this afternoon. Here are some job ads. I suggest on Monday you start looking for another job in the company. Sorry, old boy, but that is the nature of things around here now."

As Tom responded, he could feel a lump in his throat. "But why was *my* division chosen to be dissolved?"

"It was my decision, Tom. I was required to cut somewhere and your division was the least important to our department. Look, you must have known this was coming," Bill said. "I was pressured to make a decision by late this afternoon and I made it, so that's that. By the way, how's everything at home?"

Tom, filled with emotions from hurt to anger, bit his lip and replied, "Just fine, Bill. We're doing just fine." With that, Bill departed.

Stunned, Tom could hardly move his legs. He had devoted twenty years of his life to this company, saw so many employees mistreated, and now he felt he was another statistic among workers who had had their dignity stripped away from them. He could understand if the needs of the business called for disbanding his group, but did this have to happen in such an abrupt, cruel manner? Besides, Bill knew of his family troubles; could he not have shown a little compassion in his approach with Tom? As Tom drove home, he was sobbing so that he could hardly see through the windshield.

Elizabeth

Elizabeth is a secretary at a university. She is very proud of herself, for she was an immigrant with no formal education, and yet she was promoted "through the clerical ranks" to reach a secretarial position. She is proud, too, that she is able to help her husband, who is a car mechanic, support her family. She is a good secretary and is well liked by everyone in her work area.

As she was going for her routine check-up, Elizabeth's doctor discovered a small hard lump located under her arm in her left breast. The mammography and biopsy revealed that it was a cancerous tumor, and the cancer had spread to her lymph nodes. It was imperative that she have surgery to remove the breast and some of the lymph nodes. Everyone in Elizabeth's office rallied around her during this time. Many prayers, flowers, hospital visits and phone calls came from her coworkers and supervisor.

Upon her return to work, Elizabeth told her supervisor that she would be undergoing chemotherapy for three months. She said that her doctor felt it would be beneficial for her to continue to work. Her supervisor and the other people whom she supported agreed.

The first three weeks of treatment were painful for her, but Elizabeth managed to get to work and do her job as best she could. She typed a bit more slowly, and at times she needed to rest because she felt nauseous and dizzy. She also had some crying spells and moodiness. Her doctor assured her that this was temporary.

Rumors about her health started circulating at the

university. "Maybe Elizabeth is dying. If that's the case, she shouldn't be working! She is making us all feel uncomfortable," they said. Some complained that cancer patients had no right being in public for others to see how sick they were. "It gives me the creeps," one person complained, "as if death is all around us." Said another worker, "We are so busy! We need a secretary that can work full time, not run to the bathroom every hour!"

The angry words got back to Elizabeth. She was crushed. These were the very same people who had showered her with gifts when she was in the hospital, and now they were turning on her. She loved these people like family and she loved her job. Now she felt alone and hurt. The ultimate blow came when her supervisor informed Elizabeth that if she could not handle the job, she should start looking for an easier assignment – perhaps a downgrade back to clerical work. Elizabeth's condition eventually worsened, the cancer spread to her left lung, and she is now home fighting for her life.

Judy

Judy's director has been pushing her to take a field sales assignment. It would mean relocating to another state for two years, but it would also mean a substantial promotion upon her return from this assignment. Judy works in the Marketing Department in an international banking firm. The position she currently holds is a high-pressured, high-visibility one. The career pathing for someone like Judy would normally lead from her current position in marketing to a field sales assignment overseas, to a promotion back at headquarters leading a department of one hundred employees. Judy is a single woman who thus far has devoted her life to her career, hoping to reach vice president of marketing by age thirty-five. However, Judy's goals have been temporarily suspended since the illness of her father.

Judy is an only child who had a close relationship with her parents, especially her father. He has been her role model as someone who achieved success throughout his career in banking. It bothered her that she was traveling a lot and devoting so much time to her career, and not enough time to her family and her own outside interests. She recognized that her parents were growing older and needed her, yet she loved her career and was thrilled to be part of the international banking scene. However, now with the sudden news that her father was dying, Judy was beginning to reevaluate her life. She decided that since she had reached some of her career goals in such a short time at the bank, she could afford to slow down a little and spend more time with her parents. So she thought....

Judy explained her feelings to her supervisor – a man who is an Elder in her church – and why she had decided to decline the offer to transfer to a field sales assignment at this time. He listened carefully to Judy and said he understood her situation at home. Three days later he called her into his office.

"It is obvious to me, Judy, that you are making a big mistake at this time in your career. While I understand that your father is ill and you want some time to pursue your outside interests, you need to think about your future. The bank can always fly you home whenever your family needs you." He was becoming impatient. "After all, you will be supporting yourself long after your father is deceased. You turn down this opportunity," he continued brusquely, "and your chances for another one will be slim. Make your choice! I need to know right away!"

Judy remained firm, but has suffered the consequences. She is no longer on the promotable list in her department, and she is perceived as a person who takes her personal life more seriously than her career. Depressed, Judy is considering leaving the bank.

Some Initial Reflections

Stories like these three occur continually throughout the marketplace. How many of us have our own stories? How many of us have suffered because of a marketplace that is devoid of compassion? There is constant conflict between the needs of the business and the needs of people. People working in the marketplace, more than any other group in our society, tend to lack a balance in their lives. They have trouble harmonizing their inner, personal and spiritual lives with their work activities. A closer look at these three stories will show that there could have been a better way to approach each situation with understanding, compassion and kindness, while still maintaining the needs of the business.

In Tom's case, Bill, his supervisor, had to make a business decision knowing he was going to affect the lives of the people in his department, including Tom's. He knew Tom as an excellent worker who had devoted so many years of his life to the company; he knew Tom was hurting from his family troubles, and he knew the kind of man Tom was toward others. Bill knew, too, that Tom was a devout Catholic, for Bill and Tom belonged to the same parish, both serving on various parish functions together. Wasn't there a better way that Bill could have approached Tom with the bad news about Tom's job? Couldn't Bill have offered to help Tom find another job in the company? As a fellow Christian, couldn't Bill take some of those Gospel messages on love and caring that he heard at church and apply them when speaking with Tom about his decision to disband Tom's division? Was it really necessary to tell Tom the news on a Friday, knowing that he was facing an upsetting weekend with his children? What are a Christian's ethical responsibilities in the marketplace when dealing with people? Is "brotherly love" only shown on Sunday, and does it stop on Monday?

With Elizabeth's health problems, her supervisor and coworkers led her to believe that they truly understood her struggle with her illness and had openly welcomed her back to work. Three weeks into her treatment, which is not enough time for someone to adjust to chemotherapy, the people in her work environment turned on her. Gossip spread, sarcastic remarks were made, and finally Elizabeth was told that she needed to "shape up" or take a downgrade. Couldn't her office have hired a temporary employee to assist Elizabeth during her three-month treatment? The office often hired temporary secretaries during emergency work times, so hiring one now would not have been a problem. Besides, wasn't this an emergency time – an employee in desperate need of assistance? Instead of isolating themselves from her (perhaps they feared they would "catch" the disease), couldn't they have shown the same kind of compassion that they displayed while she was in the hospital by offering to help her when she became nauseous on the job, buying her a soda to ease her upset stomach, talking with her about how she felt, or just by being kind to her during this time? Many of these people were Christians, who outside the work environment took care of their families, attended church meetings and volunteered in the community. Shouldn't that caring have overlapped into their daily work lives too? How would they feel if they were in Elizabeth's position?

Regarding Judy's situation, it is almost appalling to hear how her supervisor, an Elder at her church, spoke to her. Not only did he threaten that her career would be jeopardized because of her life decisions, but he even made sure that his threats were carried out! Where was the compassion for a woman who was grieving her father's anticipated death? How could he speak so callously to her about her father and her future? Should Judy just abandon her father? Couldn't her supervisor, while concerned for the needs of the business, have told Judy that her decision to spend more time at home may mean a setback in her career, but that she need not worry, for this was only temporary, and that once her family situation was settled he would personally ensure that her career would be in full swing again?

These stories are real and happen every day in the marketplace. I know, for it has happened to me throughout my career in both the academic and the business professions. It is stories like these that moved me to write my letter on The Dignity of Work. As a Christian I felt that it was my responsibility to take a stand on our humanity in the marketplace. I was tired of watching the suffering of so many people with whom I work. I felt the call to act.

What does it mean to be a Christian today in the marketplace? Many people profess to be Christians, but how many of us really know what that means? Like the Chanel perfume television commercial, in which a voice softly invites us to "live the fantasy" as we watch the abstract visions, we need to "live the faith" throughout our daily lives, not just on Sunday. What role, then, should we play as people who "live the faith" in our working lives?

Do we, as working people, have a special ministry of our own distinct from the ministries of ordained ministers, priests or other religious?

Do we need to have special training to be ministers in the marketplace?

What is the Christian Church's position on this kind of ministry?

Jesus often told his followers not to "lord it over others," but to serve. Are we not called to serve in our work environment?

Although this book focuses on the Christian at work in the world, lay ministry in the marketplace is not reserved only for Christians. As children of God we can all unite together, Christian and non-Christian alike, in one holy ministry. It is not religion as an end in itself, but rather the act of serving others, that brings us together in union with God, which is the ultimate goal. Differences in faith lie in creeds and rituals rather than in spiritual principles. Being guided by faith is the way to true spirituality. Each child of God is called to ministry.

Being children of God in the marketplace means that we do business differently. We who are Christians have a calling to live the teachings of the Gospels in the workplace. We have a role model in Jesus Christ, who exercised most of his ministry in the marketplace. How do we do this? How do we harmonize the needs of the work environment with our calling as Christians?

The marketplace should be a place that encourages each person to express his or her own dignity. It should be a place of community. Work should be a place where we discover ourselves as well as prove ourselves. However, in many respects work does not serve that function at all, but only causes us pain and hurt. The three stories just described are examples of what each one of us has experienced at one time or another. Why is this happening today? Is the "American dream" an illusion that has gone sour at the expense of human dignity? What's wrong in the marketplace? How did we lose our sense of humanity?

Questions for Study and Reflection

1. Imagine yourself in Tom's or Elizabeth's or Judy's situation. How would you want to be treated?

2. Imagine a coworker in Tom's or Elizabeth's or Judy's situation. How would you act towards them? Would you treat them the same way that you would like to be treated?

3. Have you ever been in a personal situation similar to that of Tom, Elizabeth or Judy? Describe what happened at work. Was it generally a positive or a negative experience?

4. What do you think causes people to act as Bill, Elizabeth's coworkers or Judy's supervisor did?

5. Have you ever had a coworker or employee in a similar position to that of Tom, Elizabeth or Judy? How did you react? How did others react? Could there have been room for improvement in the way this person was treated?

Chapter Two

The Marketplace: Its Culture and Philosophy

It is not wrong to want to live better; what is wrong is a style of life which is presumed to be better when it is directed toward "having" rather than "being," and which wants to have more, not in order to be more but in order to spend life in enjoyment as an end in itself.

— JOHN PAUL II[1]

THE MARKETPLACE has been the center of community, commerce and controversy since the beginning of humankind. In the Old Testament we read about a deeply committed people working in a supportive community to achieve three common goals: worship of a single God, development of family life and survival of the race. The fundamental spiritual values of the Old Testament are:

1. obedience to God
2. respect for self
3. respect for neighbor
4. respect for environment.

The marketplace was the place where people met to exchange news and goods of the day. It was a place for people to gather to buy, sell and trade their products and services.

The ancient Hebrews considered work to be the chief area in which people expressed themselves. The Old Testament view is that "all human labor is a call from God to share in the responsibility of caring for the world. By itself work leads only to frustration, but under God it is a sharing in the blessing of creation."[2]

In the marketplace of business, then as now, the common goal was profit, and then as now it was often achieved at the sacrifice of others and the environment. In the book of Genesis God gave his people *dominion* over the world, not *domination*. In other words, God entrusted the world to his people to use, not abuse. To have dominion over the world meant living those four fundamental spiritual values. However, through greed and competition dominion became domination, and this began to undergird the free market and undermine mutual respect. It became a struggle between good and evil.

By the time Jesus was born the marketplace was corrupt and a new god had emerged on the scene, the god of Mammon. Jesus chose to do most of his preaching in the marketplace. Although the religious leaders of his day criticized him for associating with the less acceptable people in the marketplace, he recognized the need to mingle with the people. The people came to know him, to observe him, to join his company, and to listen to him speak about loving one another and about service to God through serving God's people. He warned of serving two masters and taught the Golden Rule of "doing unto others as they would have others do unto them." They witnessed his love and kindness and saw him touch a leper as he healed him. They heard him speak words of forgiveness to the paralyzed man, challenge the Pharisees to say whether they wanted him to kill or give life on the Sabbath, respond with sympathy and power to the widow of Naim, and invite the hemorrhaging woman to speak to him. They experienced his actions in the marketplace as a counterbalance to what they were accustomed to. Jesus understood that the marketplace was where he could touch the lives of the people of God. He brought good news to the suffering and the afflicted, he comforted the brokenhearted, and he taught charity and service to those who were fortunate to have wealth and power.

In many respects the marketplace today has not changed. In fact, in today's industrial and technological society it seems to have become worse. In my twenty years of working in the marketplace I have witnessed a steady decline in spiritual values. The marketplace is more competitive, more aggressive in its dealings today than ever before. By "marketplace" I mean businesses, the health care professions, teaching and academic institutions, and the entertainment industry; it is a place where people perform any task, physical or mental, for a living.

The Japanese god of never-ending work to whom individuality and personal life are sacrificed has now become a role model for corporate America. "Ironically, the surrender and detachment approach to success is anything but ordinary in business today," comments Dr. Michael Ray, professor at Stanford University Graduate School of Business and co-author of *Creativity in Business*. "The tack taken more often is a square-jawed strategy like *Winning through Intimidation* or *Power Plays to Profit*." For example, businesses are requiring employees to devote so much of their lives to their careers that little room is left for personal time, family life and God. Modern workdays and workloads require heavy personal commitments of time and energy. Work has become the most significant area of our lives. According to a survey in *Discipleship Journal* most people consider the most important aspects of their lives to be: *first*, work; *second*, family; *third*, belief in God. People are often so totally immersed in their work that they are unable to stand back and evaluate its relationship to what God wants them to do. The marketplace encourages a "better-than" attitude: *better than* our competitor, *better than* our coworkers, *better than* our neighbors – even better than ourselves, no matter what the consequences may be.

The pace is fast; the living is shallow and limited. Our fast lifestyles, fast expensive cars, fast food and fast divorces have distanced us from one another. The motto is: "Do whatever it takes to make money, because money is the key to success." In this materialistic age we measure success by the false criterion of dollars, of material things. We imagine that happiness and inner peace lie in that direction.

We are at the mercy of Madison Avenue advertisers with their campaigns and commercials depicting youthful, well-dressed, aggressive men and women climbing to the top of management by outdoing or humiliating their coworkers or competitors. Local bookstores carry a wide variety of "how-to" books that promise success in everything from how to dress, how to climb the corporate ladder, how to deal with success, and how to manage one's money. Magazines feature articles on the "good life" of materialism, and *Lifestyles of the Rich and Famous* is a very popular television show. The goal is to work for more money, more promotions and prestige, more "playthings" such as sports cars, yachts and vacation homes.

The issue of accumulated wealth in our society raises moral concerns about the rise in the homeless, medical and health care for the elderly, and unemployment among blue collar workers. Sweeping changes in the marketplace due to the massive restructuring and staff reduction that result from mergers, takeovers, bankruptcies and mode of operation of corporate life have generated an atmosphere of apprehension. People's very livelihood and dignity are threatened. Corporations, which are created and exist to serve people, instead run roughshod over them, creating powerlessness and humiliation for most of their employees with more skill than they produce products. Corporations and professional institutions ease their guilt by supporting and funding outside charities while ignoring the adage that charity begins at home.

The cost of competitiveness, among individuals and

in the marketplace as a whole, has caused ethics to take a back seat. Ethics is not principally about headline issues: ethical concerns surround us all the time whenever we deal with people in the course of the average day. High ethical standards – business or otherwise – are, above all, about treating people decently. That means respecting a person's privacy, dignity, opinions and natural desire to grow, and rejoicing in their respect for (and by) coworkers. However, we become so trapped in the web of success that we either forget what it is like to be kind, or we become too distrustful of everyone around us. We assume that everyone is our competitor and is out to ruin us.

During my first semester of teaching at a local college the chairperson of the Literature Department asked me to take over the classes of an aspiring young professor. Liz had contracted mononucleosis and would be unable to teach for one semester. She met with me twice over the summer months to show me her course curriculum for the forthcoming semester. We became instant friends and she was relieved that I was willing to substitute for her, since she feared that one of the more "seasoned" professors would be assigned to teach her classes. I was no competition for her, since I was a newly hired instructor.

Liz's specialty was remedial reading. She taught students who had learning disabilities. While I was nervous about teaching those students, I had compassion for them since I too had suffered from a learning disability known as dyslexia. Therefore I immediately established a rapport with them, and I won high praise from my chairperson for my teaching methods and my ability to reach these students. "It was really Liz's excellent course curriculum that helped," I said, trying to give Liz the credit that was due her.

Then one day in late December, while I was chatting in my office with my office mate, Liz stormed into the room. "How dare you take over my students! How dare you win over the chairperson!" she shouted.

"Who do you think you are? I thought you were my friend! You are just some young whipper-snapper coming into this school, thinking you can just take over!"

Astonished, I said, "Hold on there, Liz. I don't know what you mean."

"Oh, you don't? I have heard talk that you are sensational as a teacher in my classes, and that the students think you are great. Let's get one thing straight: I am the only remedial instructor in this college – not you. I also intend to take further action to see that you are removed." Liz ran out of the office and slammed the door shut. I began to cry. I didn't know what I had done. I taught the classes according to her instructions. I reminded the students that Liz would be back next semester. I even gave her credit to the chairperson for the success of these classes. I tried very hard not to "take over" from anyone. "Have mercy on her," said my office mate, Tom. "We are all under pressure to achieve tenure, and the department heads like to play us one against the other. It's all in the name of politics and competition. You did the best you could have done. Liz knows that. She is just running scared. You need to learn the game around here."

Welcome to the marketplace! Sometimes out of fear, some very fine people will go astray and play their company's games for fear of repercussions or loss of status.

Teachers in today's schools have the added pressure to teach business courses and motivate their students to the idea that the MBA is the ticket to success. Less emphasis is placed on literature, philosophy and thinking, while more emphasis is placed on quick study, computers, competition and the number of business degrees a student can add to his or her resume.

Hunger and homelessness are on the rise because many people cannot compete in the marketplace or keep up with the ever-increasing inflation. The stress is high for survival, especially for those who must work to earn their daily bread. We no longer have the time, energy, interest or awareness to notice or care about what is happening in our world, or to notice the destructive effects of our work environment. We lack the ability to integrate the work, recreation and spiritual aspects of our lives. Meanness has replaced gentleness.

Sally was a manager of AT&T's Stock and Bond Division. She loved her job and was well respected by both her superiors and her coworkers. She was loyal and trustworthy, kind and considerate toward everyone. Sally reported to Marie, a highly competitive woman who once advised a female employee not to have children, for it would not only ruin her body but also delay her climb up the corporate ladder. (The woman, incidentally, did have children and is now a vice-president at AT&T.) Marie was mean to her subordinates, but Sally did her best to win Marie's respect.

One warm September weekend Sally's father had an automobile accident in which he lost some toes. Sally was home at the time and flew with her father in a medical helicopter to a teaching hospital that could attempt to reattach the toes to his foot. Everything happened so quickly that Sally forgot to take Marie's home phone number to tell her that she would not be at work on Monday. While at the hospital Sally did call her friend Diane, who was a peer of Marie's. She explained the situation to Diane, and Diane reassured Sally that she would inform Marie. "Don't worry about us," comforted Diane, "you just be with your family at this time. We'll see you when you return. By the way, is there anything we can do to help?"

When Sally returned to work that week, she found a very unsympathetic Marie waiting for her. "Why did you have Diane relay your message to me?" Marie asked coldly.

Sally explained that since everything had happened so fast, she had forgotten Marie's home number and, since Diane was her friend, she had asked her to let Marie know about the accident.

"You have a mother, right?" countered Marie.

"Why did you have to stay out so long? We had a project due on Tuesday!"

From that day on, the relationship between Marie and Sally became strained. Marie ensured that Sally was not included on any special projects. She sabotaged Sally's chances for promotion, assigned more menial tasks to her, and thought nothing of belittling her in public. Sally finally had to take her cause to AT&T's EEO/Affirmative Action Group for harassment charges. Their investigation revealed that Marie was suffering from an addiction to diet pills which were causing her mood swings and personality changes. She received immediate help, but after three months in drug rehabilitation she quit the company. Marie was to be pitied. She was a victim of our materialistic society. Marie represents any one of us who is trapped in the illusion of success in the marketplace.

Christians in the marketplace are faced with dilemmas and with considerable frustration as they struggle to live in a world of shifting values. On the one hand, they have been taught to love their neighbor, respect the environment and themselves, and serve God; on the other hand, they are trained in the marketplace to be committed to doing whatever it takes to succeed, regardless of the cost. They recognize that there are moral issues involved in many of their everyday decisions and actions, but often remain unclear about how to act in a given situation. Sometimes, when they speak out about unjust or unethical treatment of others, they in turn are censured or ostracized.

"I wish I could do what you do in the workplace," said a friend of mine who works for a large corporation. "I wish I could work eight hours a day for God, but I don't have the background or education that you do to incorporate the two – work and God." Christians long to make a powerful impact at work with their faith. However, it takes no special skills or degrees to do this: it takes courage, faith and an understanding of spiritual priorities. There is nothing wrong with possessions or homes, or with striving to become successful; what is wrong is to go about achieving these goals by hurting our neighbor or ourselves, or by maintaining a false idea of what constitutes true happiness and fulfillment. Consequently, Christians in the marketplace find themselves being pulled in two directions. Many Christians believe that God and the workplace do not mix. "When I walk out the door in the morning," states one business executive, "I leave my religious beliefs and God at home. They do not belong in business."

We need to remember that the mission of Christianity is not in the church sanctuary, but in the marketplace and the community. The mission of Christianity, to influence the secular world, is outside the church walls. Christianity is meant to be lived on the street where it is rough and tough. We are called to exercise a style of leadership in the marketplace that brings out the best in others, and to minister to those in our working environment by showing concern for their problems.

Christians are challenged to live an ethically distinctive lifestyle. As Christians we must carry out our work with dedication to our employer, our coworker, our employee, ourselves – and most importantly, God. Our daily work ought to be offered as an opportunity to glorify God. Our lives should make an impact through the way we serve other people. The hallmark of our society today is to live for ourselves, but if we want to make an impact as Christians, we must do so by serving others. In this way we will realize the ultimate meaning of work and will gain tremendous peace.

Questions for Study and Reflection

1. The Psalms say, "Unless the Lord build the house, they labor in vain who build it." Jesus says, "Seek first the kingdom of God, and all these things will

be given to you." Compare this to Dr. Michael Ray's statement that "the surrender and detachment approach...is anything but ordinary in business today."
What does it tell us about the "rat race"?
How can we "let go and let God" in our workplace?

2. What can you foresee as the ultimate effects on family life in our country if the "never-ending work" ethic becomes the rule rather than the exception?
Will these effects have any impact on the workplace?
If so, will the effects be positive or negative?

3. Compare the possible negative effects of alienating or losing a highly respected employee like Sally with those of having a project delayed for a day or two due to a genuine emergency. Which, in the long run, do you think would be worse?

4. Have you ever been faced with a work situation involving ethical compromise or unfair treatment of a coworker or employee? What action did you take?

Chapter Three

A Personal Journey into the Marketplace

A healthy person must be able to work and love.

— SIGMUND FREUD

I WORK for a company of approximately 300,000 people worldwide. A company so large that its employees often refer to it as a "microcosm" of the world. A company with many different nationalities, ethnic origins and religious beliefs. A company that has experienced tremendous change in the last ten years due to the divestiture of its telephone operating companies and constant reorganization within its corporate structure. A company which has gone from being a monopoly to being a leading competitor in the telecommunications field and thus has experienced a change toward a more competitive working environment. A company known in the past for its humane treatment of and care for its employees. Yet that has changed, owing to the new corporate philosophy of "lean and mean" and "quality first."

I remember, as a little girl, shopping with my father at a well-known department store, and the salesman with whom my father was chatting asking my father where he worked. When my father told the man that he worked for AT&T, the man's eyes lit up with wonder and he said, "Oh, how lucky you are to work for AT&T. My brother-in-law works there and he loves it! I hear from him and so many of my customers who work at AT&T what a wonderful company it is and how AT&T cares for its employees!"

I saw my father's pride as the man spoke. Years later while shopping at the same department store I was asked by the saleswoman where I worked. When I told her I worked for AT&T she looked at me with compassion and said, "What a shame that nice company has joined the ranks of other corporations in this country in their meanness to their employees. So many of my customers are stressed by what is happening at AT&T and I feel sorry for them. How do you cope?"

So the public, too, saw and heard about the changes that were occurring at AT&T. However, as the saleswoman implied, what was happening at AT&T was only indicative of what was happening in the moral culture of today's marketplace.

In my wildest dreams I never thought I would be caught up in the changes at AT&T, let alone be working there! That was not my goal. From the beginning of my life I had always felt the call to serve. As a child I knew suffering and pain, having been very ill from the time I was an infant. I was also afflicted with a learning disability known as dyslexia, an impairment of one's ability to read, and I struggled throughout elementary school to overcome this disability. I had a loving family, lots of friends and people who cared, for I was a popular child with an outgoing personality. No one ever knew I was really hurting inside and alone in my suffering. Music was my comfort. By the time I was ten, I was playing piano at concert halls and school events. I could escape from the world through my music, playing for hours and hours. It brought me a lot of healing. In many ways it still does so today.

I was a deeply religious child, and at one time had contemplated a religious vocation. In fact I remember announcing after Mass one Sunday to our pastor that I wanted to be a priest! I was sensitive to other people's plights and had a gift for comforting others. Jesus was my role model through his suffering and his desire to serve people. I wanted to follow in his footsteps.

My high school years were marked by loneliness and isolation. I was not popular with the "in crowd," and went through an early awkward stage growing taller than the boys in my class. Once again I withdrew into my music. I also made an effort to reach out to those students who suffered more than I from the physical, emotional and social disabilities and inadequacies that caused them to be rejected by their peers. It was a terrible time in my life and I was glad when graduation came.

I blossomed during my college years. The Vietnam War was forcing all of us to reevaluate our country's ethics as well as our own personal and moral values. It was a time of peace, love and a return to spirituality. R.O.T.C. was out and non-violence was in. As students we rebelled against our parents' ambitions for us to "get a good career, get married and live a middle-class life." We boycotted big business, thinking it was almost a sin or "cop-out" to major in marketing or finance. I majored in English literature, hoping to continue my graduate education so that I could eventually teach at the university level. I loved college, for I felt free. My desire to serve people was encouraged during those wartime years. I was involved in many student social justice activities. I felt hope in the world. I also had an idealistic notion that this feeling would last.

My personal journey into the marketplace began when I started teaching at the university. Still feeling the call to serve, I believed that I would be able to answer this call through the teaching profession. I loved my students and they responded to me with respect and trust. However, I soon discovered that the academic environment was no different from the business world in its competitiveness among the faculty and administration. I became caught up in the competitive edge. As a young, naive college instructor I was proud of my academic accomplishments and credentials, having won the New Teacher of the Year award and published two literary articles at the onset of my career. The "older" faculty members felt threatened by my success and I was often advised to lower my enthusiasm. The competition for survival in the academic world was fierce. I was promoted from adjunct instructor to full instructor within a year, and was being considered for an assistantship position. I was a good teacher and enjoyed teaching, but I was also too busy competing for a better position and more recognition. I wanted more – more exposure, more prestige, more money.

Then my world collapsed! Two days before the fall semester of my fifth year of teaching, the secretary to the chairperson of the Literature Department telephoned to tell me that I had been laid off due to salary cutbacks at the university. All non-tenured teachers were fired. "Don't bother to show up for teaching on Monday," said the secretary nervously, "for your classes have been cancelled."

I was stunned. I made an appointment with the chairperson to find out what was really happening at the university. He was quite cold and annoyed that I had taken up his time. "What about my accomplishments in publishing and winning the New Teacher of the Year award?" I asked. "Doesn't that count for any consideration on my part?"

He was firm. "There is nothing I can do. You're young, you'll survive. I am sure you will be able to find another teaching job. Look, I have a class to teach now, so I've got to go. Good luck to you."

I was numb. I felt humiliated, hurt and violated. This treatment had robbed me of my dignity. For weeks I sat in my bedroom, unable to grasp what had happened. All my life I had wanted to teach, and now my dream was shattered. Because of the interest in teaching among my peers during those years, I was unable to find another teaching position, even with my so-called credentials. Welcome to the marketplace!

My father was working for AT&T at that time and enjoyed the environment there. He suggested that I apply for an entry level manager's position, which I did. Although I had no interest in pursuing a business career, I always had a special fondness for the Bell System since my parents, aunts, uncles and grandfather had worked there and had successful and happy careers. AT&T cared about people. It was an unusual company because its motto was "People come first," whether it meant their employees or the public. The public loved the Bell System. They could always count on it for service, regardless of the weather or the time of day. The employees took pride in working for a company that was so well respected and loved by its people, and I think that influenced the public's view of this wonderful company. I heard story after story from my family and their friends of the compassion and concern that the company showed toward their people. When my father lost his hand in a lawnmowing accident, I marveled at how the company extended itself to my father and our family during this time of sorrow with their medical, financial and emotional assistance. When my father returned to work he was greeted like a long-lost son and treated with care and love by his supervisors and coworkers. So I felt I wasn't really compromising my ideals about having a career in big business, for I felt that the Bell System was different. However, in less than two years after my entering AT&T that would change due to divestiture. AT&T would soon enter the competitive world of the marketplace.

The moral climate of our culture, however, was changing right at about the time AT&T was going through divestiture. There were no more hippies, no more peace and love. I experienced the winds of change in the little time I had worked in academia, but now it was in full bloom. A new breed had entered the marketplace – the yuppies! These young upwardly mobile professionals joined the ranks of working people everywhere and were part of the "Me" generation. Society was changing to a faster, more competitive world without any regard for social justice. I have to admit that for a time I joined the momentum.

After nine months of working at AT&T I was

promoted. I consistently won recognition awards and bonuses. I worked long hours, sometimes to late hours in the evening. I didn't have time for my family, for social justice or for caring for others, let alone for my spiritual life. When I socialized it was always with my office peers, drinking and eating too much for my health, talking about work and the "things" we now owned. As I moved up the corporate ladder, I passed close friends, not caring how they may have felt or what they thought of me. The more "things" I had or was capable of buying, the more successful I was, or so I thought.

In the midst of it all I was stressed out, unfulfilled and unhappy. I had lost touch with my humanness and my spiritual values. I was mean, but I was trained to be mean. Everyone was my competitor. Worst of all, I lost touch with who I was and with God. The extremely competitive atmosphere of the marketplace sometimes tempts us to make questionable compromises. The divestiture of AT&T and its Bell operating companies caused pain, turmoil and suffering among the employees. Employees experienced frustration, lack of human kindness, a loss of security, and most of all, an absence of human dignity. Many good and loyal people made a mass exodus to other employment, for they no longer felt themselves to be of value to the new team. Those of us who stayed were not too happy weathering the storm. The new corporate team was market-focused and market-driven, and they had little time to worry about the feelings of their peers and their employees. While much of the furor has subsided and AT&T has established itself in the competitive arena, there remained broken hearts and shattered dreams to be mended, and low employee morale to be raised.

During this time, I was changing within myself. Why was I living like this? Where was I going? What purpose was it serving for me to be killing myself and sacrificing my spiritual values for a false god? I began to resent my job, my peers, my supervisors, and the work arena in general. As a Christian I could not just stand by and watch anymore – I wanted out. I had become trapped in the illusion of the material world, and now my calling to serve humanity was haunting me.

In the course of my career at AT&T various bosses and other people had treated me disrespectfully when I questioned the ethics of some business transactions. The company was experiencing worldwide growth in the telecommunications industry, and I was growing too, only not in the same direction as the company. I stopped competing with my coworkers and put an end to those ridiculously long hours. I challenged my superiors on their treatment of employees, refused to participate in business operations or methods which would harm someone else or were unethical, and no longer socialized after hours with my coworkers in order to catch up on the latest work activities. In other words, I became an individual, which is unheard of in the corporate world.

However, I was now being labeled as a person who cared more for people than for business. So I decided that I would leave the marketplace in order to follow my calling to serve others by becoming a pastoral minister in the Catholic Church. To achieve this goal I began studying for a graduate degree in pastoral ministry at Seton Hall University. Desperately determined to leave AT&T and to escape the corporate grind, I buried myself in academic study, church activities and committees and social causes, openly condemning the marketplace and those who worked in it. I longed for the "idyllic" religious life and even gave considerable thought to joining a lay missionary order. Religious, to me, had the true vocation – they worked for God.

Toward completion of the degree I was required to do a field study project for one year. I chose to get a certificate in Spiritual Direction and Social Justice. My academic advisor, Dr. Zeni Fox, recognized my desire to serve society and thought spiritual direction would be a good choice for me. Zeni and I were close enough for me to tell her of my pain and frustration with my work life. As concerned as she was for me, she was even more concerned at the prospect of my quitting my job to pursue a ministerial life. There weren't enough church positions in pastoral ministry, she warned, nor was the pay substantial enough for a single person to support herself.

Zeni's warning only put me in a further state of despair. I was faced with a dilemma, exacerbated by my study of spiritual direction and social justice. What was I going to do with my life? I did not want to live in a world devoid of spirituality where money is the god, or to sell out my spiritual values and beliefs. I wanted a career in which I serve the people, not rape them of their dignity. I did not want it on my tombstone that "she lived and died for AT&T."

Meanwhile, life was coming to a head for me at AT&T. Reorganization after reorganization was wearing down many employees. A new buzz word hit the scene, *quality*. Quality programs were growing throughout the business world, and AT&T joined the bandwagon. Quality meant producing a good product, increased productivity and customer satisfaction. Nowhere was employee satisfaction mentioned – no one seemed to realize that happy employees are necessary in order to produce a quality product. The pressure at work only increased. Many employees felt stressed and began to become cynical about the company.

Some of the employees heard that I was studying to be a pastoral minister and counselor with a certificate in spiritual direction. Little by little, people would start to appear at my door to have a cup of coffee and to chat about their life at AT&T and in general. Some employees specifically asked for spiritual direction. I was deeply moved by their plight and humbled that they sought me out for guidance. However, I felt that I needed to do more to help them. But how? More discernment followed. I prayed and prayed.

One cold February day my mail brought me a newsletter from The Christophers, an organization dedicated to making people aware of the spiritual and social justice issues that challenge the world. Their motto is, "It's better to light one candle than to curse the darkness." The newsletter contained a letter by Father John Catoir, director of The Christophers, on The Dignity of Work. In it he addressed priests, bishops, ministers and religious on the growing lack of respect toward the church volunteer who comes to assist them in their ministerial and administrative work. He emphasized the dignity of the volunteers' work inherent in their effort to serve God and the Church. Fr. Catoir saw volunteering as a vocation which should earn respect from the people whom they assist. "We are all under pressure in our vocations," he said, "but let's take the time to treat those people who serve and work for us with dignity and love. Let's not short-cut their dignity of work."

Fr. Catoir's letter overwhelmed me. If he only knew how he lit the candle for me! It was then that I resolved to write my own letter on The Dignity of Work and send it to AT&T's magazine. Into that night I composed my letter.

"You're crazy!" exclaimed one friend. "You can get fired for writing such a letter!"

"Why?" I asked. "I'm not condemning anybody. We're all to blame, and likewise, we're all responsible. Besides, it probably won't get printed, so don't worry." I mailed the letter to the editor, satisfied with what I had done. "I did it for three reasons," I told friends: "for God, for the employees who are suffering, and for myself. I had to answer the call I felt from God to live my faith. What the consequences will be doesn't matter. I had to take a stand and I did it."

On March 14, 1989 my letter on The Dignity of Work appeared in AT&T's most circulated magazine, *Focus*, which is mailed to the home of every employee. I was delighted that this respectable and powerful publication took the risk in printing my letter (see the preface). In the letter I spoke of the decline in respecting and caring for one another. Here we are, a world-leading company in telecommunications, but no longer the leader in humanity. People don't want employee attitude surveys that amount to nothing; people want respect and love. Surveys deal with statistics, not people. The letter continued by asking questions on how each of us treats one another in our daily work activities. Charity and mercy should begin at home. Finally, I asked whether we see our work as a vocation and not "just a career": a vocation that balances work with personal life. The letter ended with the statement that competition is not synonymous with meanness toward one another.

Friends and associates were excited for me, but were cautious, too. "I hope there won't be any repercussions from your letter," worried one friend. Said a sarcastic associate, "Don't think anything will come of your letter. No one here cares about the dignity of work."

However, on March 28 a handwritten letter to me and to the employees at AT&T was printed in *Focus*. It was signed by Bob Allen, Chairman of the Board! What a wonderful surprise! Letters and phone calls from over one hundred employees began to pour into my office. Heartwarming, loving responses were expressed from all parts of the world in which AT&T employees work. Some made me cry, some made me laugh, but one thing was certain: people out there were hungering for someone to listen to them and express their feelings and concerns. "You have a ministry at AT&T," said Zeni Fox, "you are making a difference." Wrote one friend, "Please don't leave us. We need you to minister to us and to teach us how to minister to one another, for we have forgotten how to do that lately."

It didn't stop there. On May 23 *Focus* published an interview with me on The Dignity of Work and the reactions from the employees to the letters from me and Bob Allen. More letters and phone calls came. I even heard from outside companies and newspapers on what I had started at AT&T. So many people, at all levels at AT&T, wanted to join in and change the work environment.

This is a wonderful start toward lay ministry at

AT&T. I am proud to have been an influence, a minister, in initiating change, and to see how people in my company are responding to the call to serve. There is still more work and ministering to be done at AT&T. I don't want to paint a picture of a perfect world there as yet – there are still many people who resist change and scoff at the whole concept of The Dignity of Work, which means that my work there is still cut out for me. Will I leave AT&T? Will I leave the marketplace? I don't know where God will lead me. For now, I intend to stay to be AT&T's conscience, to be the voice that cries out for justice, to be the person who lights that candle of hope and dignity for others. I think the greatest compliment I could have received regarding my letter was from a security guard who, upon seeing me step into an elevator to my office, shouted, "Hey, there goes the Minister Lady at AT&T. God bless you for representing us!" With that, those in the elevator with me clapped.

> You too go into my vineyard, and I will give you what is just. (Matthew 20:4)

All these years I wondered where my calling in the world would lead. All these years I stood idle in the marketplace, worrying that life was passing me by. My ministry had been there all along – I just didn't see it as a ministry. I thought ministry meant working in a church. Jesus kept his promise about giving me what I wanted and prayed for. I just needed to go into his vineyard – the marketplace. Each and every one of us in the marketplace has a ministry to serve. We just need to be open and accepting.

Questions for Study and Reflection

1. Are you a workaholic? Is it wrong to be a workaholic?

2. Comment on the public relations value of a company's reputation for the way it treats its employees. How, if at all, is that reputation likely to affect the company's "bottom line"?

3. The book of Genesis describes how God gave the human race dominion, not domination, over the world. Can you draw parallels between our exploitation of the environment (pollution, Chernobyl etc.) and our domination of our fellow humans through competitive, aggressive behavior in the workplace?

4. "Those who confer benefits will be amply enriched, and they who refresh others will themselves be refreshed." In what concrete ways can you apply this proverb in your daily association with employees or coworkers?

Chapter Four

Representing God in the Marketplace

How many of us believe the following statements are true?
- *"Vocation" means a calling to be a priest, minister, sister or brother.*
- *"The Church" means the pope, bishops and clergy.*
- *Work is a necessary evil.*
- *To be an "active Christian" means to be involved in parish activities.*
- *Religion is about other-worldly matters.*
- *Spirituality is for professional holy people.*
- *We go to church to get away from the world.*
- *Sunday is for God and Monday is for business.*

— GREGORY F. AUGUSTINE PIERCE,
FORMER PRESIDENT,
NATIONAL CENTER FOR THE LAITY

BEING GOD'S representative in the marketplace is another way of saying "lay ministry." The term "lay ministry" refers to God's high calling to faith and to service. Christianity had its roots in what we now call "lay ministry." The early Church knew no dichotomy between clergy and laity – that distinction came much later. In the primitive Church all were "laity"; the ordinary people were the backbone of the Christian movement. Taking fishermen from their boats and nets, Jesus made them fishers of human souls.

He dared to believe that ordinary people could become extraordinary servants of God. He

> would build his church upon believers like Peter. From among the common people he would call disciples who in turn he would send to disciple the nations. In our time it may be that the greatest single bottleneck to the renewal and outreach of the church is the division of roles between clergy and laity that results in a hesitancy of the clergy to trust the laity with significant responsibility, and in turn a reluctance on the part of the laity to trust themselves as authentic ministers of Christ, either in the church or outside the church.[1]

We, the laity, the people of God, are called to build God's Kingdom on earth. We are called to give witness to Christ throughout the world. This is called an *apostolate*, a Greek word meaning "to be sent" as on a mission. Christ sends his faithful ones into the world to transform the values of society and individuals into those of the Kingdom of God, to minister to people as he himself would minister.

Unfortunately, however, the tendency still exists to think in terms of traditional divisions of labor and specialization between clergy and laity, with the clergy in a more active, the laity in a more passive role. We the laity need to shed our reluctance to trust ourselves as authentic ministers of Christ both in and outside church, and to recognize and accept that ministers of God are found in every vocation and profession, not just in ordained ministries. We need to establish a clear sense of our own identity as a ministering people, each one called, empowered and gifted by God to continue the work of Jesus in our world. The "world" thus becomes the place and the means for the lay faithful to fulfill their Christian vocation, because the world itself is destined to glorify God the Father in Christ. "The lay faithful are not called to abandon this position that they have in the world," states John Paul II.

For many people, "lay ministry" still connotes primarily "churchy" activities, or such recognized service professions as pastoral ministry or hospital chaplain. Yet all followers of Christ, whatever their occupations, are called to his ministry – to be his representatives. Ministry is a response to the needs of others, whether those needs be personal, corporate or societal. We are called to become involved with others in their needs. For us, the laity, the world – the marketplace – is where our real ministry takes place. It is not easy in the marketplace; yet it is there that we find our calling, there that we find our identity, there that we will receive power.

In the workplace the Christian lives not only for self and family, but also for neighbor, community and world. These are the ideals from the Hebrew Scriptures that were the roots for Christianity referred to in chapter two. In the workplace God's people are called to live a sacrificial love, to challenge the prevalent spirit of self-interest, and to do justice.

> The reality of servant ministry for everyone else is filled with hard realities: getting and keeping a job, running a family, maintaining a house, and relating redemptively to neighbors and to the world community. They must confront and respond to the difficult questions of life every day: What would Jesus do in this situation? What is happening to our world? How can I tell a co-worker that I care?[2]

Whatever may be in doubt about the Christian worker's role, there can be no doubt that he or she is called to a caring ministry. We must offer to people in need the comfort, strength and guidance which comes from God. We must be concerned for the well-being of our fellow workers. In that place in which we spend most of our waking hours – namely, our place of employment – we are called to witness to our faith at all times. No area of mission is more demanding than the marketplace, in terms of ethical challenge or involvement with people in their varied needs.

As Christian workers we bear the enormous and

awesome responsibility of living out our faith before a world which is quick to seize on our failures. As lay Christians in the marketplace we can directly affect the future patterns and quality of work life, either through our own personal decisions or by participating in those organizations (such as AT&T's Work Relationships Support Team) which contribute to those decisions.

Living an active spiritual life, then, is not only for professional "holy" people like pastoral ministers, hospital chaplains and spiritual directors. We are all called to be God's representatives in the marketplace. What empowers us for such a task?

1. We are empowered as laborers. It is through the unique character of our vocation as laborers in the marketplace that we find our calling. As lay faithful and laborers we are members of Jesus' working order, for he himself labored as a carpenter doing his Father's work. Jesus is the vine and we, as Christians, are his branches (Jn 15:5). As lay faithful we are the laborers in his vineyard. Our labor matters to God. Work has instrumental value as a means of loving and serving God and others. We become coworkers with God in the everyday tasks of our work life. St. Paul enjoins us, "Whatever you do, work at it with all your heart, as working for the Lord, not for others, since you know that you will receive an inheritance from the Lord as a reward" (Col 3:23-24). When we see work in this light, we fulfill the highest destiny to which anyone can aspire – we become partners with God in accomplishing God's work in the world.

Work is a means to several ends:

- Through work we love people by serving them
- Through work we meet our own needs
- Through work we meet our family's needs
- Through work we earn money to give to others
- Through work we love God.[3]

God gave humans dominion, not domination, over the world. This means that we are created to be coworkers with God in caring for the world (Gn 1:28) through our work. We are God's coworkers in the world not by dominating but by caring. When we care for others, we find ways to work for their genuine good, and we bring out the best in them. We do well in serving God by understanding that God is active in us and works through us in resolving most conflicts between ourselves and the workplace.

2. *We are empowered by the Holy Spirit.* The Holy Spirit gives a vast variety of charisms, inviting people to assume different ministries and forms of service and reminding them that what distinguishes persons is not an increase in dignity, but a unique, individual capacity for service.

> The word *charism* denotes the gifts bestowed by the Holy Spirit on any member of the body of Christ for the building up of the community and the fulfillment of its calling. The word *ministry* in its broadest sense denotes the service to which the whole people of God is called, whether as individuals, as a local community, or as the universal Church.[4]

Each of us has our own unique charism, and each charism has its purpose in God's plan.

> There is a variety of gifts but always the same Spirit; there are all sorts of service to be done, but always to the same Lord; working in all sorts of different ways in different people, it is the same God who is working in all of them. The particular way in which the Spirit is given to each person is for a good purpose....All these are the work of one and the same Spirit, who distributes different gifts to different people just as he chooses. (1 Cor 12:4-7, 11)

Jesus relied on the Spirit while he was on earth as the source of his power for teaching and ministering. Christ taught that we all would continue his ministry when the Spirit came. After the resurrection, Jesus promised to send the Spirit to those who believe in him. He promised that the Spirit would be in them. The Holy Spirit will teach, guide, enable, and be the living link between the believer and God.

> Because Jesus incarnated Himself in each believer, there can be no lifting up of some as more significant than others. There can be no higher calling than that of bearing Jesus about in our mortal bodies to express His continuing presence in the world. Distinctions between "clergy" and "laity" become totally meaningless when every Christian realizes he is stamped with the presence of his Lord.[5]

The lay faithful are empowered by the Spirit as members of Christ's body to participate in achieving this goal through their own special ministry. We live "in the world" through our professions and work. We live "in the world" through family and social life. The challenge for us is to find spiritual meaning in our work. The marketplace is filled with people who are unhappy, unfulfilled and searching for answers to their personal and spiritual questions and problems. We have a mission to be disciples of Christ in the workplace: to love and help our neighbor; to live by the Gospel teachings; to be like "beacons of light" and follow Christ's example as laborers in God's vineyard.

Lay ministry matters to God. It has intrinsic value, like all good gifts to us from God, and it has instrumental value as a means of loving and serving God, others and our families. Looking at lay ministry this way can revolutionize our attitudes and behavior at our workplace. Perhaps we will see how what we do all day relates to God's plan. In other words, we will become coworkers with God in the everyday tasks of life.

The calling of the people of God is a high calling. The responsibilities are overwhelming. Answering this call means finding ways to answer Jesus' challenge to love our neighbor, to feed the hungry, to educate the ignorant, to make peace, to counsel the bereaved. It means doing these things where we spend most of our waking hours – on the job.

> Thus it's vital to see in Scripture that the [people] of God are more than a new covenant people, kingdom people, and servant people. We are also *empowered* people. God's Holy Spirit, always the agent of enablement, has taken up residence in the life of each believer.[6]

Questions for Study and Reflection

1. Evaluate the statements listed by Gregory Pierce at the head of the chapter. Do you believe that any of them are true?

2. What does it mean to "challenge the prevalent spirit of self-interest" in the marketplace? In what specific way can you do this in your own work life?

3. "In one body we have many parts, and all the parts do not have the same function....Since we have gifts that differ according to the grace given to us, let us exercise them."
   St. Paul in his letter to the Romans is telling us that we each have our special gift, and each gift has its own special place. How do you see this in your own work situation?
   If you believe this to be true, then to what extent (if any) is competition with your coworkers necessary? To what extent is it necessary for you to "lord it" over your subordinates?

4. We frequently hear the word "enabler" these days, usually with the negative connotation of someone who (consciously or subconsciously) helps someone to continue a dysfunction such as alcoholism. But God's Spirit is the agent that *enables* us to do God's work on earth.
   How can you *enable* an employee or a coworker to realize their highest potential on the job?
   What will be the consequences if you do this: will your own position be threatened; will the business suffer; or will the consequences be positive ones?

Chapter Five

The Dignity of Work

Letter to the Editor of AT&T's Focus *Magazine on March 28, 1989:*

Regarding Dee Dee Torrell's letter on The Dignity of Work, I commend its reading to all the people of AT&T! Ms. Torrell has put the right balance and perspective around the job – or the work – and the essential "humanity" that we must achieve in our relationships with each other. Being competitive and caring about each other are not mutually exclusive. In fact, combining the two guarantees our success.

— BOB ALLEN, CHAIRMAN OF THE BOARD

"YOU ARE making a difference," said Dr. Zeni Fox. "Go and read what *The Lay Members of Christ's Faithful People* has to say about lay ministry. You may be surprised that you are doing that already at AT&T. Perhaps, too, that is why you are still at AT&T. Perhaps God needs you to do a ministry there."

The Lay Members of Christ's Faithful People by John Paul II answers the question, "What role do the laity play in the Church?" It is a question asked by the laity in all Christian faiths. Those in ordained ministry and in religious life are automatically connected to the Church in their daily work, but as more and more lay people become active in their churches and seek to be more involved, how do they fit in? What is the nature of their ministry?

"The 'world' thus becomes the place and the means for lay faithful to fulfill their Christian vocation," writes John Paul, "because the world itself is destined to glorify God the Father in Christ."[1] It is through their labor, their daily work, that lay people have their opportunity to exercise their special vocation of ministry in the marketplace. The laity are situated in the secular world, and it is there that they are called by God. The laity live in the world, that is, in every one of the secular professions and occupations. The laity must see their daily activities as an occasion to join themselves to God, fulfill his will, serve other people and lead them to communion with God in Christ.[2]

Despite Zeni's encouragement I still felt unsure about my purpose in working for this major corporation. "I want to work in an environment where I am needed, where I can do God's work and serve humanity," I told a business friend.

"But don't you see?" said my friend. "You have a ministry *here* – a special ministry all your own. People here are poor too, poor in spirit. The marketplace has robbed them of their dignity. Look at that letter you wrote on The Dignity of Work. It reached 300,000 people! Don't you think you touched some hearts with that letter? You certainly touched the heart of Bob Allen. Look at the responses you received. And now you want to leave! You touched my heart. You got me thinking differently on how I approach and work with others, and you made me more aware that I can combine my spiritual and business lives at AT&T. Why not stay and teach others?"

My friend convinced me. I chose to stay at AT&T to expand my ideas on The Dignity of Work, and to develop and implement The Dignity of Work principles for my business associates at AT&T and in the marketplace. I am beginning to see the effects of the principles of The Dignity of Work upon my company.

What does "The Dignity of Work" mean?

To most people The Dignity of Work means the right to paid employment and a safe and decent workplace. To others it means medical and pension benefits, meaningful work and proper career pathing.

To be a human person includes the right to work. Jesus, himself a man of work, a craftsman like his foster father Joseph of Nazareth, knew and understood this right to work. Jesus belongs to the working world. He has an appreciation and respect for human work.

While The Dignity of Work certainly encompasses the ideas of paid employment, meaningful work and benefits, it goes beyond that. The Dignity of Work includes human dignity in our relationships with one another in the marketplace. To discover the importance of conducting business with compassion and honesty instead of with deception and meanness is to acknowledge and practice The Dignity of Work.

"Wouldn't it be wonderful," asks Gregory F. Augustine Pierce, former President of the National Center for the Laity, "if Christians were noted for the way they conducted themselves at work with others?" It would be wonderful. Unfortunately, that is not what is happening.

A friend of mine, Chuck Jones,* vice-president at one of AT&T's competitors in the telecommunications industry, was recently transferred from the engineering department to a smaller division with less responsibility and prominence. His only "fault" was that his mentor had retired from the company and left Chuck and some others vulnerable to the new corporate regime. Chuck received word of his transfer during a business trip to Japan, via a telephone call from his new president. He was told to report for work at his new division on the Monday of his return. "Now when I enter the board room for our monthly officers' meetings, my peers fumble around as to who will sit next to me. Some of those peers were also my friends. We used to socialize together with our families. Since my transfer they act as if I have the plague! No one wants to be seen with me. It is as if I have fallen from grace, and it hurts! I feel I have been treated shabbily by my superiors, my peers and my friends."

Too many of us in the marketplace have experienced this rejection. Too many of us are hurt by

*Name has been changed

and dissatisfied with our jobs because we work in an environment that feeds into a corporate machine which grinds out profits and productivity without any care for the human person. "What I did learn from this experience," said Chuck, "is not to treat the people reporting to me with lack of respect for who they are as people. I do wonder whether what happened to me could have been an outcome of how I may have treated people in the past? You know that Gospel saying, 'As you sow, so shall you reap'? It has really made me think."

We are often caught up in the politics of competition and striving and, like Chuck, we forget who we are as people; we forget the sensitivity and feelings of others, and we forget to respect them. We are so busy with our own work that we no longer have a balance between work and personal life; between work and social justice; between work and spiritual values. The marketplace fails to foster spiritual values.

What are those spiritual values? They can be summed up by the Golden Rule:

> Do to others whatever you would have them do to you. This is the law and the prophets. (Mt 7:12)

To treat people with kindness and understanding, with honesty and integrity, and with respect for their dignity as a human person is a spiritual value that can and should be incorporated into our daily activities in the marketplace.

Good people management does not sacrifice the needs of the business for people's needs. Meeting the needs of others creates a better climate for meeting the needs of the business. This not only leads to more satisfied workers, but it also reduces poor quality work and increases operating effectiveness. Few of us take the time to "reach out and touch someone," as the AT&T commercial jingle says. In the workplace the best intentions slip away. The Dignity of Work includes seven principles for working Christians to use in their daily work relationships. These seven principles are:

1. Do business with a heart.
2. Trust and be trusting.
3. Be compassionate.
4. Be kind, be honest, be kind.
5. Listen with a "third ear."
6. Be supportive.
7. Be of loving service to others.

** One: Do Business with a Heart **

Michael Russell, founder of the *American City Business Journal* which publishes thirty-six business newspapers in the USA, says that "there is no more powerful force on earth than love. It's the greatest power. In business, before you can ever succeed, you must have that love – of your employees, of your company, or of yourself. Implicit in all this – in loving your company and your competitors, in letting go, in protecting your opponent and just in generally doing business with a heart – is trust. Trust in others, trust in the universe, trust in God, and in the truth you know, and you will succeed." We need to learn to think with the heart, not just with the mind. "It's not our institutions that are corrupt and bad," comments Michael Murphy, director at AT&T, "it's our hearts!"

We must put ourselves in the other person's shoes. Are we helping or hurting anyone by our business decisions? People must come before productivity. That doesn't mean we should neglect the quality of our work or our product; it does mean that we must put people first in order to be successful. Quality of work and employee satisfaction go hand in hand. Thinking with a heart means paying attention to the needs of the people we encounter each work day. Because God's top priority is people, we must develop a heart for people, too. When God is in our lives and our business, we place others' interests and needs before our own. It is impossible to serve God and not serve people. Loving people, seeing the good in them and knowing that each person is important and has his or her job to do in the divine plan is part of doing business with a heart.

Here is one actual example of how a major computer corporation did business with a heart. Recently this corporation had to downsize its employee population. Rising operating costs and the decrease in revenue due to the competition from the newly united Germany meant that these cutbacks were essential to the company's survival. However, instead of just "laying people off with severance pay," this corporation acted with its heart. The executives held a series of forums with their employees in which the reasons for the staff reductions were explained. The corporation offered special retirement incentives to employees fifty years of age or older with twenty-five or more years of service. All promotions and hiring of new people were frozen so that any vacant positions could be filled with surplus employees, and for those employees who could not be relocated or who were ineligible for the retirement package the corporation established an Outplacement Program. This program assisted the surplus employees in updating their resumes, career planning and development outside the corporation, and retraining. This corporation treated their surplus employees with dignity, respect and love. No one was abandoned.

In one of our divisions at AT&T there is a poster hanging on the hallway wall that says, "We think with our hearts!" What a wonderful way to come to work each day and see that poster! We certainly know the marching call of that group. In my own division we have made our logo for posters, business stationery, calendars and conference themes, "Think people!" That philosophy is echoed throughout the division and we truly live by it. The results of this kind of attitude among both divisions have produced happy employees doing quality work. The employees feel loved and appreciated – and they are! No one wants to transfer from either group. Of how many people can it be said that they want to stay in their current employment situations?

** Two: Trust and Be Trusting **

Trust is more than just a word. It is a working climate that says we depend upon each other for our success, and because of that dependency we need to feel open with one another. Trust means respect. I remember taking a course on the Hebrew Scriptures and hearing the professor mention four qualities which, in the Hebrew Scriptures, defined a person who could be trusted: respect for God, respect for neighbor, respect for the environment and respect for self. We need to create an atmosphere of trust through interacting, communicating and working with others. An atmosphere of open communication creates a valuable two-way flow of ideas and the opportunity for people to play a role in shaping their destiny in the workplace. Trust also comes from inner peace, from being the kind of person who can live at peace with others. Inner peace is not found through outside avenues or by living on the surface of life. Inner peace comes from within ourselves and our relationship to God. Inner peace comes from relinquishing our self-will or motives, our attachment to our egos and the material word, and our aggressive thinking and action. Inner peace comes through working for the good of all. Trust in God brings us inner peace, too. No one can find inner peace through working by or for oneself, but only through having God as one's partner in the marketplace.

Having God as our partner means letting God have the ultimate control. Most of us want to be "in charge" on the job and thereby to feel the power of ownership. As one young manager said to me, "I get great satisfaction out of knowing that I am in control of this department." Consequently many of us become self-driven and self-centered, and leave little room for including or acknowledging the input, feelings or talents of others. The risks of being in total control are high, for when mistakes are made or business decisions go awry and we lose control, then we go "out of control" and blame ourselves for our failures or, worse yet, blame others.

When we have God as our partner in our work, God helps us to keep all aspects of our working lives "under control." With God as our partner our business decisions will include those moral, humane and ethical principles in our work that are lacking in today's workplace. The key element in this partnership is trust in God. Just as God trusts us to do a good job and to treat his people with dignity and respect, so, too, do we need to trust God in our daily work and business decisions. How do we do that? By giving up total control and allowing God to become part of our work plans and activities.

> For I know the plans I have for you, plans to prosper you and not to harm you, plans to give you hope and a future. (Jeremiah 29:11)

Linda's experience shows the business benefits that can be reaped from trusting in God. Linda was put in charge of a group of word-processing clerks who had an "attitude problem." These clerks had had a series of supervisors who were out to make their "claim to fame" with upper management and therefore did not remain long enough to develop these clerks professionally and give them, too, an opportunity to move up in the corporate ranks. Because of their relationships with their past supervisors these clerks were angry, resentful and not about to trust Linda. Upper management labelled them "our problem." So Linda was caught between pleasing the two groups, the word-processing clerks and upper management. She explained what happened:

> I could have taken total control of the situation by coming down hard on the clerks' attitudes with threats of transfer or lay-off if they didn't change, which is what upper management was

> looking for me to do. That would not have resolved anything, except to make me look good in the eyes of my superiors. But these clerks were people too, with the same career hopes, goals and aspirations that we all have. Wouldn't it be better all around if I could help them, change their attitude and make them feel better about their work, themselves and the company? It would be better for all involved – the clerks, upper management and the company as a whole. However, I didn't know where to begin. So I turned the whole situation over to my partner, God. If I wanted to gain the trust of my clerks as well as of my upper management, I had to trust in God to guide me. God is my consultant.

Each day as she walked into her office, Linda began the morning with a prayer to God to help her to do her best for those people. She asked God to lead her in the right direction and to bless all the parties involved. Then she started to listen to the complaints of the clerks. Some felt abandoned by their former bosses; some felt they were discriminated against because they were "just clerks," and others felt that their situation was hopeless, so why should they try to work hard?

> So with God's help I initiated a career planning program for the group. Two of the clerks wanted careers in computer programming, so I sent them for special training. Two others wanted careers in marketing, so I had them enroll at an evening marketing degree course at a local university. One clerk already had a college degree but lacked networking skills, so I helped her by calling some managers I knew in the area which interested her, and asked them if they could spend some time with her and possibly consider becoming a mentor to her. I also made them feel that they were important to the company because they provided a vital word-

> processing service. I had them view the people who came to them for their services as their clients who needed them. Many of their clients didn't know how to type or edit reports, and depended upon the word-processing clerks to complete the task. Within a year I had gained respect and trust from the clerks. I had the reputation among the word-processing clerical pools as the supervisor who cared. Their attitude changed, and with that came a new self-esteem for each one of them. My upper management was not only pleased, but began implementing my career planning program across all the word-processing pools. Everyone was amazed at my accomplishment, but I wasn't amazed at all. I knew that with God as my partner I would be successful. It all comes down to trust – letting go and letting God.

Linda's story shows how trust in others, trust in God and trust in ourselves will bring us success.

** Three: Be Compassionate **

Is someone with or for whom you are working having a "bad" day due to some heartache, pain or frustration in his or her working or personal life? Does someone need a little understanding? Compassion is more than just being helpful or doing favors. It involves a basic understanding of the needs and desires of others. Compassion is more than just an attitude; it is a type of behavior. We need to see ourselves as teachers of love and peace. No greater opportunity for expressing this kind of behavior can be offered than the opportunities to be found in the marketplace. Caring for all whom we meet and refusing to regard anyone as an instrument for our own goals is compassion. That attitude of compassion and caring extends to our family, our neighbors and the environment. Compassion means love. How often do we belittle, blame and even ridicule others, destroying their self-esteem? St. Paul exhorts us, "Never let evil talk pass your lips; say only the good things people need to hear, things that will really help them" (Ephesians 4:29).

Bob Boles, manager of a local bank, explains how a compassionate attitude benefitted himself and the business as well as an employee:

> One of my people was having trouble understanding a new computer package our department had just implemented. He could not grasp the concepts and was becoming a nervous wreck. I knew he was a good worker, so I was puzzled by his inability to learn the new software. One day I asked him out for lunch and we spent time chatting about his problem. He revealed to me that he had dyslexia which causes problems in understanding concepts. He was too ashamed to tell me in front of everyone in the office. Had I not taken the time to have lunch with him and to try to understand his cause for nervousness, I would never have known his problem. And it is resolvable! I now have him attending special reading and concept classes which have helped him tremendously. A little compassion on my part went a long way in the long run for my employee, for myself and for the business.

My director at AT&T has begun "Breakfast Over Business" meetings once a month with his people. "We not only discuss the needs and problems of the business," he explains, "but we find time to chat about our own lives, business or personal. Through these meetings I have gained a real compassion for what people bring to their work, whether it is because of personal problems at home or on the job. It is a time when I get to know my people as people, and not just as workers."

Try to become a source of strength and love for people. Be a role model of a person who is able to combine work and compassion in the marketplace. Put yourselves in the other person's shoes. How would you want to be treated?

** Four: Be Kind, Be Honest, Be Kind **

We can achieve more with a little honey than with a lot of vinegar. A "thank you" to a secretary or coworker will go miles. One of AT&T's executives wrote an open letter to his division which was sent desk to desk, expressing his "love and thanks to all of you who have supported this organization during our most crucial time the last three months. I love you all," he wrote. This is the same division that designed the poster, "We think with our hearts!", so the employees did not object to working overtime during those three months. They knew that their efforts would be appreciated and rewarded.

President George Bush speaks of making our country a "kinder, gentler America." I envision a gentler marketplace, whose adage is, "Be kind, be honest, be kind," as Doug Greene, publisher of *Delicious* magazine, coined the phrase. We should watch how we speak to people, and we should be decent and polite in our dealings. Above all, we ought to have integrity and honesty – which goes hand in hand with trust and being trusted too.

How many of us conduct our work with honesty and integrity? Ethical concerns surround us all the time whenever we deal with people in the course of our average day. Ethics is about treating people decently. The Book of Proverbs says, "Dishonest gain will never last, so why take the risk? Because the wicked are unfair, their violence reverberates back unto them and destroys them" (Proverbs 21:6-7). Kind and honest relationships are hidden assets. Good relationships also create that elusive asset called good will, and will sow the seeds of future success. When this is understood in the marketplace, when kindness, honesty and integrity are included in our working relationships, success is achieved on every level. This includes increased profitability, greater customer and employee satisfaction, and a real contribution to the community and to society.

** Five: Listen with a "Third Ear" **

"I always listen with a third ear to my patients' complaints," states Larry Goldfarb, Doctor of Chiropractic Medicine. "This means that I go beyond hearing their physical complaints. Perhaps their physical ailments may be due to something deeper that is happening to them, such as stress at home or work. Perhaps not, but at least I try to search if there is an underlying cause to their physical problem."

Listening with a third ear is hearing beyond the sound of words that our ears pick up. It is being open to the intuitive sense of listening with our hearts and minds. What is it that your coworker, subordinate or customer is really saying? They want success and happiness as much as you do. Listen to their needs.

A division manager at AT&T started a new program entitled "Families Are Important," a program that was dedicated to restoring family life in the marketplace. "Over and over again I heard the complaints of my employees about how they were tired of working for a company who cared little about family and personal life. It was beginning to reflect not only in their attitude, but in their work. I held focus groups within my division to hear what they were saying – and what they were saying was that their families were feeling neglected and excluded from the employees' work life. So with much thought and meditation, I decided to develop this program where families are invited to visit the workplace every quarter throughout the working year and be part of the work team. We also have a newsletter that includes social and family events and announcements. This is mailed to every employee's home to share with their families. The results have been remarkable. The complaining has stopped and the employees seem happier. It's a start, anyway." Because this division manager was able to listen beyond the complaints of her employees and put into action their inner desires, she achieved success.

** Six: Be Supportive **

Christians in the marketplace should be deeply committed to working in a supportive "community" to achieve company goals. Be enthusiastic. Be a team player and encourage others to be a part of that team.

"My administrative staff complained to me in a meeting that they did not feel part of the team. They felt of less importance than the medical staff," commented Bob Geller, Vice President of Human Resources at the Kessler Institute for Physical Rehabilitation. "Little things, they felt, sent messages to them that they were second-class citizens, such as reserved parking for the medical staff and punching time cards each day by the administrative staff only. So I made a decision to eliminate both at Kessler. At first the medical staff objected, especially to the removal of their reserved parking spaces, but when I explained how important the administrative staff are to the successful working operations of this hospital, and that without them administrative and personal work would not get done, they calmed down."

This is not an unusual instance. When it takes the employees of a large corporation twenty minutes to find a parking spot because many of the spots are reserved for the executives who are often away, that certainly sends the employees a message of "second class" citizenship!

A "game plan" or market strategy that major companies use is the "win/win" strategy. This means that through quality of work, dedication and perseverance the customer wins, and so do the company and its employees, with more profits, productivity and customer satisfaction. While this strategy may be valid in principle, it is often achieved at the cost of human dignity. The competition becomes intense and fierce, business ethics and values drop, people are disillusioned, distressed and dissatisfied. At the most it is a "win/lose" strategy, and at the worst it becomes a "lose/lose" proposition. However, through using the principles of The Dignity of Work and adopting a game plan of teamwork, fairness, compassion and purposefulness, we can make everyone a winner. Many of us think of winning simply in terms of getting more than we already have or getting more than someone else. The goal of the win/win way should be that everyone involved wins. We need to look at each situation in terms of "you *and* me" rather than "you *or* me." We need to let go of concern for our personal prestige and to recognize that everyone on the team has a vital role to play. Further, we need to view competition not as an invitation to destroy our competitor, nor as a justification for envying them, but rather as an opportunity to learn from them and a challenge to energize ourselves to do our own very best. Competition should keep us on our toes and excite us to strive to be that much better, while acknowledging that there is room in the world for our competitor as well as for ourselves.

Competition need not be synonymous with meanness. Competition does not have to be destructive. We can succeed in supporting each other as human persons part of a team, a working community, in the marketplace. Work and competition can be fun and healthy when compassion, support and kindness are blended into the competitive edge.

** Seven: Be of Loving Service to Others (*Diakonia*) **

This is the most important principle of The Dignity of Work. Diakonia means service. *Diakonia* is a Greek word meaning "to wait at a table or to attend to a person's bodily needs; to render service to another person." It is impossible to serve God and not serve his people.

> For I was hungry and you gave me food. I was thirsty and you gave me drink, a stranger and

> you welcomed me, naked and you clothed me, ill and you cared for me, in prison and you visited me.... Truly, I say to you, as you did it to one of the least of these, you did it to me. (Matthew 25:35-36, 40)

Jesus speaks clearly about tending to the needs of others through loving service. Businesses and institutions discharge their responsibility of serving others through providing financial contributions to outside charities and organizations, but loving service means giving of oneself and sharing life with those around you. Service to others is about loving in the midst of brokenness; it is about being an instrument of grace at a time of uncertainty; it is a commitment to walk with others, wherever they may lead, and it is allowing oneself to become attuned to the God within others and in oneself. The principle of Diakonia is so vital that the entire following chapter will be devoted to it and will include some examples of people who are practicing Diakonia in their work environment.

To sum up the principles of The Dignity of Work, the workplace should encourage every individual to express his or her own creativity, potential and the human dignity that is the right of all people. We can support and help one another to do good work so that everyone becomes successful. To work in a pleasant, purposeful environment is everyone's right, where "productivity through people," not "productivity through profit," is the motto.

"To me being a Christian person in the marketplace simply means treating students and staff where I teach as human beings with needs and wants just like me," states teacher David Gurica. "Taking a positive attitude about my job and showing enthusiasm for what I am doing is a way of demonstrating my convictions. I have made it a point to get along in a genuine way with all my students and coworkers."

The activity of AT&T's Consumer Products (CP) organization is a true "success story" showing the Dignity of Work principles in action. CP has developed the Shared Values theme which has infused new energy into the employees who work there. Their symbol is the Shared Values pyramid which is displayed throughout the organization.

The essential ingredient in the Shared Values that serve as the foundation of CP's business and the basis of their success is love.

"Using love in this context is a bold step, but I think we're ready to legitimize the 'L' word and put love into our business," states CP's President Ken Bertaccini. "We are talking about love in the context of love your neighbor as you love yourself, and treat others as you would like to be treated. We don't hold to the scenario that there's no room for love in business. We all need to love one another to exist individually and collectively whether it's on a personal or a business level. Adding love to our Shared Values challenges us to own and live our personal values of caring, trust and respect. Certainly these are all definitions of love. You can't care for someone, trust or respect them if you don't love them. And putting love in our Shared Values pyramid sends a message to our people and to everybody, inside and outside of AT&T, who looks at Consumer Products that we do care about each other. We wanted to clearly and consistently establish these Shared Values as the foundation of our business."[3]

The words "owners" and "people" on the sides of the pyramid recognize CP's individual commitment to owning and living those values, while the base of the pyramid acknowledges the customers as the critical foundation of the business.

The results of CP's success are staggering! Consumer Products was cited as a role model by AT&T's Corporate Officers for all of AT&T's business units. Their employee turnover is minimal, many of the employees seeing themselves more as part of a "family" than just as members of a work group. "It is as if you are supporting a member of your family in achieving success," explains one CP manager.

"We take pride in our success and pride that each one of CP's employees is successful. We are a 'good

Our Shared Values
OWNERS
PEOPLE
CUSTOMERS
EXCELLENCE
QUALITY
COMMITMENT
INNOVATION
TRUST
INTEGRITY
CARING
LOVE
RESPECT

news' story that should be told to all who are in a competitive business," states another CP employee. CP's market share is up and they are continually favored over the competition. Their technology, market focus, customer commitment, financials, and operating style present a tremendous lesson and learning mechanism for all businesses. States one CP product manager, "Our customers like dealing with us. They see us happy in our work. They like our attitude. They know that we care about our employees and about them. They know that because of this Shared Value philosophy they are going to get the best product they can get."

Concludes Ken Bertaccini, "Our Shared Values are, and will continue to be, the source of our strength and our success. They enable us to be the best for our owners, our customers, and our people."

The Dignity of Work should not just be so many words or a meaningless motto, but a way of life. Improving our work relationships with people puts into practice the concept that people are important. The respect, dignity and care given to all people in the marketplace elicits in return increased respect and care for the well-being of the business. This leads both to increased personal fulfillment and to increased prosperity for the business. In the beginning I undertook to write the letter on The Dignity of Work as an expression of my frustration with and concern over an environment that lacked respect for me and others as human beings. Now I see it as a small step in helping others to have the courage to make changes in their working lives. Every good deed we do, every good word we say, vibrates from one person to the next. One person can be a light in the darkness. Work is a way of offering ourselves to God by being a light to his people.

We have the power to choose: to be happy or unhappy in life; to serve others or to avoid them; to make a difference in this world or to remain indifferent to the world's concerns. There are many other choices we can make about our work. If we feel spiritually unfulfilled in our work we can choose to quit our jobs – a choice, however, which most of us cannot afford to make. Or we can remain in our jobs and compensate for the lack of fulfillment by becoming involved in church activities or volunteer work. Or we can learn to glorify God by treating our work as an opportunity to make a difference through cultivating a spirit of service for others. Through living the seven principles of The Dignity of Work we can achieve success, fulfillment and enjoyment in our work, our working relationships and in our spiritual journey with God. How shall we choose?

> For what does it profit a man to gain the whole world and forfeit his life? (Mark 8:36)

Questions for Study and Reflection

1. "One sort of friend is a friend when it suits him, but he will not be with you in time of distress....A faithful friend is a sturdy shelter; he who finds one finds a treasure" (Sirach 6:8, 14). What kind of friends did Chuck Jones have in his work situation? What can you see as the consequences of being a "faithful friend" to a colleague like Chuck Jones?

2. "Quality of work and employee satisfaction go hand in hand." Evaluate this statement in terms of your specific work situation.

3. Imagine that you have some kind of problem with your coworkers or employees, for which you are seeking a solution. Imagine yourself:
   - putting yourself in their place, seeing the problem from their perspective
   - praying for them.

   How do you think this will influence the way you come to solve the problem?

4. Suppose that Bob Boles had decided to fire and replace the employee who had trouble learning the new computer software. What would have been the consequences in the workplace? In the long run would this have been a more or a less costly way to deal with the situation?

5. In what specific way can you "be kind, be honest, be kind" in your workplace?

6. How can you generate a positive "team" atmosphere at your job?

Chapter Six

The Seventh Principle: Diakonia

The Son of Man came not to be served, but to serve.

(Mark 10:45)

DIAKONIA IS a call to all believers to serve the needs of the whole Church and the needs of the wider community.

"I am not a Christian, but I feel I serve the needs of the community by the way I conduct my work," states Larry Goldfarb, Doctor of Chiropractic Medicine. "I am a deeply spiritual man and I try to use those spiritual values I was taught in my religion, which is Judaism, in serving those in my practice."

Before Larry starts his day, he prays in his office for God's blessing and asks to be a channel of God's healing energy as he works on each patient who comes to his office. "But I go the added mile to serve, too. I educate each patient on good health and healing. I recommend further treatment with a specialist if the circumstances present themselves, but I will then call the specialist myself and make the appointment for the patient because I know how unnerving and scary it can be to know one needs additional medical care. If a patient cannot pay me for some reason, I will waive the payment. Often what happens is that the patient will give me vegetables from her garden or he will fix my plumbing for free. No matter, I don't look for the payment, but somehow it all works out. God is my partner in my practice."

Larry has also served the people who work with him. He meets with his associate partner and the receptionists each week to hear their needs and resolve any problems they may have in the office. "All four of us are of different faiths, but we start off each meeting with a prayer. We care for each other and they know I care very deeply for their feelings and concerns. At our meetings we reaffirm the goals of the office. I make sure we have a good time in this practice. We certainly have a family-like atmosphere. So I feel I am serving all the time. I like the word "Diakonia" and what it means, but does it only apply to Christians?"

Diakonia does not only apply to Christians. The spiritual message and principles discussed in this book can apply to all believers in God. Religion is not an end in itself; it is the act of serving others that brings us union with God which is the ultimate goal. Differences in faith lie in creeds and rituals rather than in spiritual principles. We are all part of the same race, the human race, and we are all part of the same family with God as our Father and Mother.

However, it is true that Diakonia is associated with the works of Jesus Christ. Jesus' whole life was a diakonia of humankind. Jesus was *the* diaconal human being. "Of his own free will he gave up all he had, and took the nature of a servant" (Phil 2:7). Jesus is the model of service because he made choices of self-giving and self-sacrifice rather than allowing society to dictate his behavior. He was the true Servant of God who came not to be served but to serve and to give his life for humankind.

Diakonia is often associated with service to the poor. Diakonia is serving Christ, who himself calls us to help the poor. Yet Diakonia is not just for the materially poor, but for the poor in spirit as well. The marketplace is full of people who are poor in spirit – people who are so involved in their work and the "needs of the business" that they have lost sight of the problems, suffering and needs of others with whom they interact on a daily basis. How can we practice Diakonia in the marketplace?

"By giving of ourselves and helping others, they become an extension of who we are and they cannot take away from what is already yours and mine," explains Marie Santana, Administration and Personnel Director in the Federal Government Affairs Department at AT&T. "The spiritual world and the marketplace should be integrated into one whole person." Marie is not professionally qualified in ministry or counseling, but she is a pioneer in serving the people at AT&T. "The call to serve has always been with me. I try to give of myself to others as Christ did. I try to live my faith," she says. In addition to her daily work as Administration and Personnel Director, she helps to foster the careers of employees by offering mentoring programs at AT&T and throughout the marketplace. She has developed such a high reputation for success with her mentoring programs that she is considered a professional consultant on mentoring in the field of Human Resources. She gives her services for free and she is in great demand from businesses, academic and medical institutions throughout the East Coast. Marie believes, "Although mentoring is a corporate word, I feel it is also a spiritual word, for mentoring is ministering to others in the marketplace."

In her mentoring programs Marie is more of a teacher than a lecturer. She teaches people how to help guide and nurture the careers of others, through caring for the business and personal needs of those being mentored. She offers herself as a facilitator, friend and mentor to those who attend her sessions, giving personal attention to each person there. With every program she has started, she has formed a new community, "another extended family," as she puts it. "I ask myself each day, do I really invite people into my living room? Do I really want them to be a part of me? The answer is always yes, if I am to follow Christ."

Besides individual efforts, like Marie's, toward service to others in the marketplace, organizations can

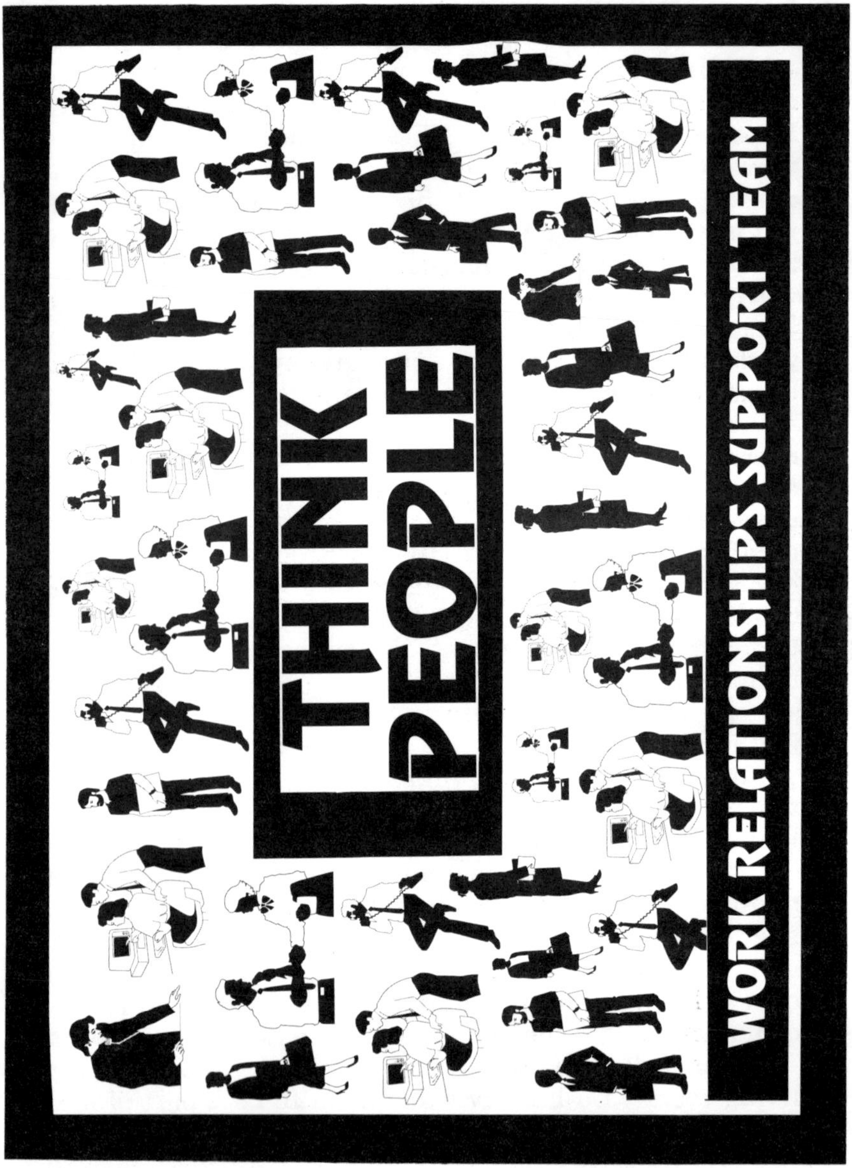
THINK
PEOPLE
WORK RELATIONSHIPS SUPPORT TEAM

also join in the call to Diakonia. In my own division, Marketing Services, we have implemented a program called the Work Relationships Support Team (WRS). It was begun in 1984 by Larry Garfinkel, Vice President of Marketing Services, as a committee dedicated to surveying the employees within the division about problems, concerns and frustrations in personnel and the overall operations of the organization. The results of the survey would then be presented to the Vice President in an attempt to resolve some of the problems. Some resolution was achieved, some things fell by the wayside. After I wrote my letter on The Dignity of Work, Larry invited me to become a member of this committee and asked the committee to update its purpose to serve the needs of the division. Through the guidance of Mike DelCasino, Chairperson of WRS, and the WRS members, the committee became a team, with a mission to serve the people within the division. The mission statement reads as follows:

> Work Relationships Support (WRS) is a Marketing Services Organization (MSO) concept designed to maintain, on an ongoing basis, MSO's commitment to the quality of work life and the needs of our employees, not only as workers, but as people. This includes quality of performance, integrity, honesty, work ethics, and the dignity of work.
>
> The WRS Team is dedicated to promoting and maintaining these values as an inherent part of MSO's day-to-day working relationships. We view ourselves as change agents, sincerely interested in making MSO the best place to work. This team fosters an environment of teamwork, communication and employee satisfaction that will contribute to AT&T's winning in the marketplace.

The WRS motto is, "Think people." States division manager Mike DelCasino, "It is Diakonia in action.

WRS serves the people. It is truly people serving people. WRS is people getting together, on a voluntary basis, with the intention of airing incipient problems before they become real problems."

WRS is a service concept, fostering service programs and ideals. "With all the recognition awards programs at AT&T for outstanding achievement in work, WRS is unique because we have a Humanities Award for outstanding human service in the work environment. We do not evangelize or preach humanity to our people whom we serve, we act on it," continues Mike, who is known as a caring manager to his own people. "People don't give simple values or ideas credit. Simple things like being fair and caring to each person you meet goes a long way. I don't believe you need to get involved in complex ethical issues to make headway in serving people. In my own way of managing, I look at people not just as employees, but as people. I always consider what people must do in attempting to get their work done, and sometimes it can be frustrating or unpleasant for them. Being an active member of WRS has heightened my sensitivity toward working people's problems. I serve the people by being fair, open and honest in my relationships with them and by serving as Chairperson on WRS."

Through word of mouth from employees at AT&T on the success WRS has had in the Marketing Services organization, the WRS team has been asked to help start other WRS teams within AT&T and in the outside business community. It is a concept that is growing widespread in the marketplace. I am proud to be a member of this winning team!

Jesus enjoins us not to lord it over others (Matthew 20:25-28; Mark 9:34, 10:42; Luke 22:24). In the marketplace we must ensure that this does not occur. "I look upon Jesus' statement about not lording it over others as not unlike parenting," says Katherine Bakes, dance professional, actress and teacher. "My goal is to make actors successful and like a loving parent ask for nothing in return when that success comes. I do not lord over them as if I were some 'guru' or master who was instrumental in their achievement, nor do I expect them to owe anything to me. Then it no longer becomes a loving service; it becomes an ego thing instead."

Katherine also believes that she is serving the acting community by her example of moral and spiritual living since the entertainment world is full of "immorality, lack of kindness and sharing," as she sees it. "You think the business world is dog-eat-dog? Try working every day in the entertainment world where competition and cut-throat maneuvers are the norm. I serve as teacher, counselor, minister and mother to these actors who are wounded after a day's work. It is a never-ending service."

"People don't see their work as part of their spirituality," comments Michael Murphy, Director of Business Communications Services at AT&T. "They see work as socially valuable and important. I think we delude ourselves in thinking that way." Michael is another Christian worker living his faith through Diakonia. "We are called to service by Christ. We are called to witness. I don't do much testifying at work, but I do see my activities at work as serving God and his people."

Being a Christian does not automatically make a good manager, and likewise, being a good manager does not mean he or she is a spiritual person. "But being Christian, we have been endowed with special spiritual gifts," says Michael, "and Diakonia is a gift as stated in Romans 12 and 1 Corinthians 12. I do not worry about how successful I will be on my job, that's God's business. I worry about how I served the people I work with during my busy day. My faith affects the way I work with people and I am conscious of the things I do for them. I give thanks to God for them and for the opportunity to serve them. I pray each morning for a servicing sense, a witnessing sense to Christ."

Stella Wilkins is a German immigrant who knows suffering. She remembers coming to America from

Germany and trying to acclimate herself to the new culture. She felt alone, for she was ignored or mistreated by people because she was considered different, an outsider. Being exposed to various jobs in the marketplace taught Stella how cruel the world can be. As she grew in success, she was determined to treat people with consideration and fairness, something which was not often given to her.

"Diakonia is a beautiful word! I work in a service career as a librarian, and I love it, for it gives me the opportunity to serve people every day," explains Stella, who is a librarian at the Immaculate Conception Seminary at Seton Hall University. "I use your principles on The Dignity of Work in my job. I counsel and interview each person that comes to do research in the library, and I listen with a 'third ear' as to what their needs are in finding that right book or material in completing their research. I don't just say, 'Look it up in the card catalog,' but I make myself accessible to them. I get a kick out of their faces when they have found the exact information they have been searching for."

I have had the pleasure of Stella's service. Many times I have come to her in desperation, because I did not know where to begin in researching material for a term paper or class project. Stella is always there, reassuring and offering her services to me in finding the right information. I attribute much of my academic success to Stella's service.

"I feel I am part of the research team. I even love to follow up with students, professors and professionals on the outcome of their research projects," states Stella. "God has given me so many gifts, so I owe it to God to do good work and serve him." Stella's office is also open and welcoming to her coworkers and students at the university. Stella feels she also owes her coworkers consideration, honesty and fairness. She concludes, "I help them find and discover themselves. I try to be an example of a person who trusts God and lives her faith." Stella is the most sought-after librarian at the university. She has been a gift of service to others.

God is love, and whenever we reach out in loving service to others we are expressing God. Loving people, seeing the good in them and their potential, and knowing that each one is important and has a job to do in the Divine Plan is permeating everything with God.

"I can't be responsible for the will of God; I can't be responsible for people's behavior; but I can be responsible for my actions," states Bob Ettl, District Manager at AT&T. "I am conscious of how I treat people, and since your letter on The Dignity of Work was printed, I have become more conscious of it."

Bob Ettl has had a twenty-year career at AT&T and is a part-time instructor in business communications at a local university. "I once had an employee work for me who was demoted, not due to his poor work habits, but due to external circumstances. In fact, at one time he was on the same management level as me, so coming to my district was a really humbling experience for him. He really didn't have the exact skills I was looking for in the job he took in my group, but I saw this as a gift from God to take this man 'under my wing' and help him regain his confidence once again. I made a moral judgment to serve and to work with him so that he could feel good about himself. I was worried that he might have been destroyed by the whole ordeal, but I remember the times God was there for me in unconditional love and service, so it was my turn to help someone in their time of need."

Bob's efforts have borne fruit, for the employee he served grew in his skills and knowledge of the job and is currently rated promotable within the department. "I get choked up when I think I may have had a hand in shaping the destiny of this man. I felt the employee had gone through enough pain and my heart went out to him. I am so proud of him!" smiles Bob. "There is a level of risk when helping others, especially in the marketplace. Not everyone is responsive to serving others. It is often looked upon as a weakness, but to be a Christian is to live Diakonia in every aspect of one's life."

I have made some personal changes on my job in order to serve people better. I did such little things as making my office a place of warmth and welcome. My office also reflects my personal and spiritual beliefs through the paintings on the wall and other items in the room. People regard it as a place of shelter from the busy work grind. In addition, I have made it a point to answer personally every letter and phone call received on The Dignity of Work, and encouraged each person I responded to by stating that everyone can play a vital role in changing the consciousness of the marketplace. Some of the letters and phone calls asked for advice or assistance with a personal or business matter. I serve them by calling a particular expert in the area of business concern, or a counselor or minister for assistance if the problem is one of a personal or spiritual nature. I share with people my life experiences and how I managed to resolve a pressing situation. Perhaps hearing my story will help them in resolving their problems. Everyone knows my office door is open for counsel, prayer or just for casual conversation. Sometimes a loving word or spiritual inspiration will give them comfort. Everyone also knows my spiritual standards and that I try to live by those standards in my daily work activities. Everyone knows I live by Diakonia, that I serve them and work for God. It has not always been easy for me. I battle every day with people who accuse me of being too spiritual or too caring – yet being "too spiritual" or "too caring" does not make a person less of a businesswoman or a less conscientious worker in the marketplace.

A manager once snapped at me, "All this service to others can go too far. You can help others, and then turn around and find that you have just been kicked in the head. You have to look out for yourself in the marketplace." There is always a risk in helping others. Jesus took that risk and he was crucified for it. However, his reward was resurrection with the Father in heaven and eternal life for all of humankind.

Although I have been hurt in serving others and have felt alone at times, I don't look for my reward from the people I serve. I know my reward will come from God. Jesus came not to be served, but to serve, to live out on earth the life of unconditional love and obedience to God.

I think that the most touching story of Diakonia comes from the mail clerk, Harriet, in my building. Harriet is a simple person who expresses herself in a simple way. She has a high school education and no particular management skills. Harriet does not care about image or making an impression. She does her work delivering the mail to each office on her floor and does it well. However, at each stop she makes it her point to chat with each person she serves.

"Sometimes I just give them a kind word or a warm smile," she says with a glow. "Sometimes a person may be rude to me or even growl at me, but I try not to be hurt by it. I still smile and say something nice to that person and guess what usually happens? That person finally can't help cracking a smile or even admitting he or she is having a bad day. Some even feel they can confide in me, which is nice. I am not knowledgeable in psychology or religion, but I offer them whatever advice I can give. I always think, 'How would Jesus react to their problems or stories?' and that's probably all the knowledge I need to help them. I have a service job, but I look upon my service to others beyond my daily work."

One day we heard that Harriet had been in a serious car accident. The halls on my floor were filled with concerned, very upset people who had tears in their eyes at the thought that Harriet might be too injured to return. "What can we do?" people asked me. "You're a pastoral minister, what do you suggest?"

"I suggest you follow your hearts," I responded. So they did. Cards and flowers filled Harriet's hospital room. Visitors from every level of management and non-management took turns sitting vigil at her bedside. Although Harriet was Methodist, an ecumenical service of healing was offered and attended by the employees on her floor. When she returned part-time to work, the employees she served were serving her. Some pushed her mail cart from office to office, while others got her lunch from the cafeteria so she wouldn't have to walk too far or stand in line. Still others offered to drive her to and from work each day and shop for groceries if she needed them. It was an outpouring of love and service. People felt good at what they had done for Harriet. "You can honor Harriet further," I commented, "by continuing your service of love and caring to all employees you interact with daily. Don't let it begin and end with Harriet. Extend Diakonia to others."

Harriet taught us all an important lesson on how to serve others in the marketplace. On her return to full-time work, Harriet passed out bookmarks in everyone's mail basket that read:

One Person Can Make A Difference.
Your efforts might seem insignificant to you
But they may be all that is needed to bring
A warm smile and comfort to someone in distress.
Take courage and follow your heart.

That's Diakonia in action in the marketplace!

Questions for Study and Reflection

1. Chiropractor Larry Goldfarb "goes the added mile to serve." What are the advantages to practicing this attitude in business? What specific advantages can you envisage in your own work?

2. Who are the "poor in spirit" in your own work environment? What can you do to minister to them?

3. How can the "mentoring" process be used to inculcate spiritual values?

4. Recall a special time or times in your life when you experienced the presence of God's unconditional love. Did God show this love through the actions of other people? In what ways can you minister God's love through serving others in your workplace? How would you regard this as a rewarding experience for yourself?

5. "Being 'too spiritual' or 'too caring' does not make a person less of a business person or a less conscientious worker." Evaluate the truth of this statement.

6. Our qualifications to be ministers in the marketplace are "our own disappointments, expectations, hopes and frustrations in the workplace." What specific "qualifications" have you experienced? In what ways could you put your "qualifications" to use for the benefit of others?

Postscript

The spirit of the Lord God is upon me,
because the Lord has anointed me;
He has sent me to bring glad tidings to the lowly,
to heal the brokenhearted,
To proclaim liberty to the captives
and release to the prisoners,
To announce a year of favor from the LORD
and a day of vindication by our God,
to comfort all who mourn. (Is 61:1-2)

You yourselves shall be named priests of the LORD,
ministers of our God you shall be called. (Is 61:6)

THESE VERSES from Isaiah tell us that God anointed all of us to serve as ministers to his people. That includes Christians, Jews, all of the People of God. Just as ordained ministers, priests and other religious are called by God to serve their churches or temples, so are we lay people called to minister in the secular world. God has placed us in the marketplace so that we can minister to our coworkers.

The ministers in the marketplace are in a unique position. What better way to serve God than by going out into the marketplace and ministering to his people? Jesus knew this. That is why he spent relatively little time in the Temple, synagogues or places where the elite gathered, and instead spent most of his time in the marketplace of his day, associating with and befriending the less acceptable and less "religious" people.

Do ministers in the marketplace need degrees in theology or pastoral ministry, or certificates in spiritual direction to qualify for their calling? No! Our qualifications are our own disappointments, expectations, hopes and frustrations in the workplace. Nothing can help us better to understand the disappointments, expectations, hopes and frustrations of those we meet through our daily work. No formal qualifications are required – just a loving heart and a willingness to serve, common sense and compassion.

> Blessed be the God and Father of our Lord Jesus Christ, a gentle Father and the God of all consolation, who comforts us in all our sorrows, so that we can offer others, in their sorrows, the consolation that we have received from God ourselves. (2 Corinthians 1:3-4)

It is not easy being a minister in the marketplace. In fact, at times it can be lonely and frustrating, even tiring. There are going to be people who will not agree with our spiritual standards, or what AT&T's Consumer Products organization calls Shared Values. There will be people who will refuse to change. However, the challenge is there to be like Christ, ministers to those who work in the secular world, who are poor in spirit and weary of the games in the workplace. We can help shape a better marketplace where all people are winners. Competition usually means meanness. Instead, let's make competition mean cooperation. Building a kinder, gentler workplace begins with each one of us. One person *can* make a difference! I did! Each and every one of us in the workplace is called by God to become his ministers in the marketplace. Will you accept the challenge?

Notes

CHAPTER ONE

1. Pope John Paul II, *The Hundredth Year.*

CHAPTER TWO

1. Pope John Paul II, *The Hundredth Year.*

2. Lawrence Boadt, *Reading the Old Testament* (Mahwah and New York: Paulist Press, 1984), p. 255.

CHAPTER FOUR

1. Robert B. Munger (Fuller Theological Seminary), in Lawrence O. Richards and Gilbert R. Martin, *Lay Ministry: Empowering the People of God* (Michigan: Zondervan Publishing House, 1981), p. 13.

2. John Sundquist, "Ministry of the Laity in the Workplace," in Baptist World Alliance General Council, *Commission on the Ministry of the Laity*, Nassau, Bahamas, July 10-16, 1988.

3. Doug Sherman and William Hendricks, "Does your job matter?" in *Discipleship Journal* 8, no. 3 (May 1, 1988), p. 24.

4. World Council of Churches, *Baptism, Eucharist and Ministry*, Faith and Order Paper 3 (Geneva: World Council of Churches, 1982), p. 21.

5. Richards and Martin, *Lay Ministry: Empowering the People of God*, p. 41.

6. Ibid., p. 147.

CHAPTER FIVE

1. Pope John Paul II, *The Lay Members of Christ's Faithful People (Christifideles Laici)* (New York: Daughters of St. Paul Editions, 1988), p. 36.

2. Ibid., pp. 36, 37.

3. "Love recognized as a shared value: Legitimizing the 'L' word in our business," in *Consumer Products Challenge Magazine* 107 (AT&T, Parsippany, NJ: July 1989), p. 2.

For Further Reading

Beale, Lucy, and Rick Fields. *The Win/Win Way. The New Approach to Transforming American Business Life.* New York: Harcourt Brace Jovanovich, 1987.

Cousins, Evert H. "Experiencing God in the marketplace," in *New Theology Review,* vol. 2, no. 2, May 1989.

Dreyer, Elizabeth. "Four reflections: The Christian in the workplace," in *New Theology Review,* vol. 2, no. 2, May 1989.

---"Toward a spirituality of work," in *New Theology Review,* vol. 2, no. 2, May 1989.

Droel, William L., and Gregory F. Augustine Pierce. *Confident and Competent: A Challenge for the Lay Church.* Chicago: ACTA Publications, 1987.

Jaffe, Dennis T., and Cynthia D. Scott. *Take This Job and Love It.* New York: Simon and Schuster, 1988.

John Paul II. *On Human Work (Laborem Exercens).* Boston: Daughters of St. Paul Editions, 1981.

---*The Lay Members of Christ's Faithful People (Christifideles Laici).* Boston: Daughters of St. Paul Editions, 1988.

---*The Hundredth Year (Centesimus Annus).* 1991.

Marciniak, Ed, Michael Novak, John A. Coleman and Sargent Shriver. *Challenge to the Laity.* Huntington, IN: Our Sunday Visitor, 1980.

McDermott, John. "The weakness of American Catholicism," in *Chicago Studies,* vol. 28, no. 1, April 1989.

Pierce, Gregory F. Augustine. "A spirituality that makes sense to this worker," in *Chicago Studies,* vol. 28, no. 1, April 1989.

Pierce, Gregory F. Augustine, editor. *Of Human Hands: A Reader in the Spirituality of Work.* Chicago: ACTA Publications, 1991.

Ray, Michael, and Rochell Myers. *Creativity in Business.* New York: Doubleday, 1989.

Rush, Myron. *Lord of the Marketplace: Putting Biblical Principles to Work in Your Business.* Wheaton, IL: Victor Books, 1988.

Second Vatican Council. *On the Apostolate of the Laity.* Washington, DC: United States Catholic Conference, 1965.

Sherman, Doug, and William Hendricks. "Does your job matter?" in *Discipleship Journal,* vol. 8, no. 3, May 1988.

Soelle, Dorothee, with Shirley A. Cloyes. *To Work and to Love: A Theology of Creation.* Philadelphia: Fortress Press, 1986.

Thomson, Bill. "Spiritual values in the business world," in *Yoga Journal,* Jan./Feb. 1988.

Work Relationships Support. AT&T: Marketing Services Organization/WRS Team, 1989.

Other Titles Available from Resurrection Press

His Healing Touch *Michael Buckley*	$7.95
Of Life and Love *James P. Lisante*	$5.95
A Celebration of Life *Anthony Padovano*	$7.95
Miracle in the Marketplace *Henry Libersat*	$5.95
Give Them Shelter *Michael Moran*	$6.95
A Path to Hope *John Dillon*	$5.95
The Healing of the Religious Life *Faricy/Blackborow*	$6.95
Transformed by Love *Margaret Magdalen, CSMV*	$5.95
RVC Liturgical Series:	
Our Liturgy	$4.25
The Great Seasons	$3.95
The Ligurgy of the Hours	$3.95
The Lector's Ministry	$3.95
Behold the Man *Judy Marley, SFO*	$3.50
I Shall Be Raised Up	$2.25

Our Spirit-Life Audiocassette Collection

Celebrating the Vision of Vatican II *Michael Himes*	$6.95
Hail Virgin Mother *Robert Lauder*	$6.95
Praying on Your Feet *Robert Lauder*	$6.95
Annulment: Healing-Hope-New Life *Thomas Molloy*	$6.95
Divided Loyalties *Anthony Padovano*	$6.95

Resurrection Press books and cassettes are available in your local religious bookstore. In case of difficulty, or if you wish to be on our mailing list free of charge for our up-to-date announcements, please write or phone:

Resurrection Press, Ltd.
P.O. Box 248
Williston Park, NY 11596
(800) 892-6657